FILE COPY
DATE 8/78

PUBLISHERS PRESS
1900 WEST 2300 SOUTH
SALT LAKE CITY, UTAH 84119

D1792322

Research Studies in Library Science, No. 13

RESEARCH STUDIES IN LIBRARY SCIENCE
Bohdan S. Wynar, Editor

No. 1. *Middle Class Attitudes and Public Library Use.* By Charles Evans, with an Introduction by Lawrence Allen.

No. 2. *Critical Guide to Catholic Reference Books.* By James Patrick McCabe, with an Introduction by Russell E. Bidlack.

No. 3. *An Analysis of Vocabulary Control in Library of Congress Classification and Subject Headings.* By John Phillip Immroth, with an Introduction by Jay E. Daily.

No. 4. *Research Methods in Library Science. A Bibliographic Guide.* By Bohdan S. Wynar.

No. 5. *Library Management: Behavior-Based Personnel Systems. A Framework for Analysis.* By Robert E. Kemper.

No. 6. *Computerizing the Card Catalog in the University Library: A Survey of User Requirements.* By Richard P. Palmer, with an Introduction by Kenneth R. Shaffer.

No. 7. *Toward a Philosophy of Educational Librarianship.* By John M. Christ.

No. 8. *Freedom versus Suppression and Censorship.* By Charles H. Busha, with an Introduction by Peter Hiatt, and a Preface by Allan Pratt.

No. 9. *The Role of the State Library in Adult Education: A Critical Analysis of Nine Southeastern State Library Agencies.* By Donald D. Foos, with an Introduction by Harold Goldstein.

No. 10. *The Concept of Main Entry as Represented in the Anglo-American Cataloging Rules. A Critical Appraisal with Some Suggestions: Author Main Entry vs. Title Main Entry.* By M. Nabil Hamdy, with an Introduction by Jay E. Daily.

No. 11. *Publishing in Switzerland: The Press and the Book Trade.* By Linda S. Kropf.

No. 12. *Library Science Dissertations, 1925-1972: An Annotated Bibliography.* By Gail A. Schlachter and Dennis Thomison.

No. 13. *Milestones in Cataloging: Famous Catalogers and Their Writings; 1835-1969.* By Donald J. Lehnus, with an introduction by Phyllis A. Richmond.

Milestones in Cataloging

Famous Catalogers and Their Writings, 1835-1969

Donald J. Lehnus

Introduction by
Phyllis A. Richmond
Professor of Library Science
Case Western Reserve University

1974

LIBRARIES UNLIMITED, INC., LITTLETON, COLO.

Copyright © 1974 Donald J. Lehnus
All Rights Reserved
Printed in the United States of America

Library of Congress Card Number 73-94030
International Standard Book Number 0-87287-090-1

LIBRARIES UNLIMITED, INC.
P.O. Box 263
Littleton, Colorado 80120

ACKNOWLEDGMENTS

It is with great pleasure that I acknowledge my indebtedness to Dr. Phyllis A. Richmond, who spent much time discussing ideas and problems, and poring over the preliminary drafts. Her interest, helpful suggestions, constructive criticisms, and patience at every step along the way, contributed immensely to the completion of this investigation.

A special acknowledgment must be extended to Dr. Conrad H. Rawski, whose influence, guidance and wisdom have inspired me greatly.

Sincere thanks and deep gratitude are also in order for Dr. Thomas G. Morris and Dr. Jesse H. Shera, who also gave freely of their time and ideas during the months spent on the research and writing involved in this study.

A particular expression of appreciation and acknowledgment has to be given to Dr. Tefko Saracevic, who implanted the seminal idea for this inquiry and encouraged me to develop it.

Also, heartfelt thanks must be given to the staffs of the libraries which were the principal sources for this study, *viz.*, the Cleveland Public Library, the New York Public Library, the Library of Congress, and the libraries of Case Western Reserve University, Columbia University and the University of Chicago.

Last, but not least, and perhaps too often taken for granted, but sincerely appreciated and continuously utilized during the course of this investigation was the *National union catalog.*

D. J. L.

TABLE OF CONTENTS

INTRODUCTION	ix
CHAPTER I—The Problem and the Methods Developed to Study It	1
CHAPTER II—The Raw Material of the Study: Definitions and Parameters	7
CHAPTER III—An Overview of the Total Constructed Network	13
CHAPTER IV—Analysis of the Most Frequently Cited Works and Their Authors	20
CHAPTER V—Interrelationships Among the Most Cited Authors: Individuals	30
CHAPTER VI—Interrelationships Among the Most Cited Authors: Institutions (Data)	44
CHAPTER VII—Interrelationships Among the Most Cited Authors: Institutions (Analysis)	53
CHAPTER VIII—Miscellaneous Relationships Among the Remaining Most Cited Authors	59
CHAPTER IX—The Time Dimension of the Most Frequently Cited Works	64
CHAPTER X—Conclusions	77
APPENDIX I—The Most Frequently Cited Works	93
APPENDIX II—The Most Often Cited Authors	113
APPENDIX III—Uses and Analyses of Citation Patterns: A Select Bibliography	117
BIBLIOGRAPHY	127
GENERAL INDEX	129
PERSONAL NAME INDEX	132

INTRODUCTION

Every true research study begins with a problem, but this problem is not always immediately defined by the person undertaking the research. Initially he sets himself the task of "looking into" an area of potential interest. As he becomes more familiar with it, he finds unanswered questions or unfollowed trails of evidence. Very often there are no guides—or guides are nebulous—so that he has to choose his methods as the problem is revealed more and more clearly.

In the case of the present study, Dr. Lehnus was interested in applying a method—in a non-standard way for that method—to a type of literature that had not been addressed so far. He proposed to begin with a single monograph on the subject "cataloging," apply the method of citation analysis to the references of that work, and determine whether a core literature on cataloging could be discovered in this way. There are innumerable examples of core literatures in scientific fields obtained from journal articles or through the *Science citation index*, but research via the monograph in non-scientific subjects has been minimal.

By back-searching each cited item until there were no more to search, Dr. Lehnus was able to create a "fan" or "world-line," resembling a genealogical chart of antecedents, covering a period of 128 years. This "fan" consisted of 7,209 citations, representing, since there were overlappings, 2,532 individual works. The frequency distribution followed the standard Bradford-Zipf-Mandelbrot hyperbolic curve, indicative of high frequency citation for a very few items with citation only once for the vast majority. Dr. Lehnus narrowed his field to a group of 184 works written by 132 personal and corporate authors. He did this by selecting a frequency of eight citations as his cut-off point. One can increase or decrease a core literature's size by raising or lowering the cut-off point. That is, the core would be smaller if a frequency of ten citations were chosen as the basis for inclusion or larger if the cut-off point had been reduced to five citations. The core literature of 184 works was the first dimension of his study.

When the core had been determined, both the works and their authors were analyzed intensively. For the works themselves, analysis followed standard patterns, indicating source, dates, type of publication, language, publisher, and so on. In the case of personal authors, the methodology of quantitative collective biography (prosopography) was used. Through the quantitative approach to biographical data, supplemented by a search of news items and similar sources, Dr. Lehnus discovered and was able to demonstrate a long chain of professional relationships stretching from approximately 1835 to the present. He was also able to show that there existed a time series of "invisible colleges" (in the sense that Diana Crane uses the term[1]). The continuing patterns of interrelationship over time comprised the second dimension of the study.

A third dimension turned up when the duration of citation was examined. Thus, it was possible to identify works as classics if they had been continuously cited over a period of 50 to 74 years, and as superclassics if they had been cited for over 75 years. Dr. Lehnus has been able to predict which works will almost certainly be cited again every time there is need for catalog code revision. The *Report* of the Commissioners of the British Museum (1850), for example, has been cited for a period of over 118 years, and it shows no signs of losing its force. He was also able to identify predecessors and successors, sources that flourished for a time and then died, and sources that now appear to be moribund. This time dimension forms a third aspect of his study. Both dimensions—personal interrelationship and duration of citation—are significant additions to the process of citation analysis.

The value of this study as a contribution to library science lies primarily in the new knowledge uncovered through the adoption of methodologies from the fields of information science and quantitative history. The factor of citation duration may have been hinted at by scholars studying the growth rates of scientific literature, but this duration does not appear to have been used heretofore as a specific means of identifying classical contributions in a subject field. While citation of earlier works by later ones makes an automatic historical pattern as well as a genealogical one, the discovery of a series of groupings of writers over a period of time would seem to be new. The degree to which authors were acquainted with one another through association in their occupations and organizations was unexpected. One would venture so far as to suggest that it now appears that it would be unusual for the leaders in a field—those writing the core literature—to be unacquainted with each other or not in communication with each other. From now on, it seems most unlikely that a scholar will be able to make a polished study of a core literature without also taking a good look at his authors and their relationships with one another.

The final smooth and logical organization of a research monograph disguises the obstacles, blind alleys, uncertainties, and dark hours of discouragement that occur before a breakthrough. Considerable perseverance is needed to bring such a study to a successful conclusion. As a counterbalance, however, one has the satisfaction of knowing that those who undertake similar research in the future can no longer successfully limit themselves to the scope and methodology previously used.

                                  Phyllis A. Richmond
                                  Professor of Library Science
                                  Case Western Reserve University

---

1. Crane, Diana. *Invisible colleges: diffusion of knowledge in scientific communities.* Chicago, University of Chicago Press, 1972.

CHAPTER I

THE PROBLEM AND THE METHODS DEVELOPED TO STUDY IT

INTRODUCTION

It has only been during the past two decades that much serious attention has been focused on the study of citations and their analyses in attempts to identify and evaluate important contributions to a subject literature and/or significant research in a subject area.[1] The *Science citation index*[2] has undoubtedly made a tremendous impact on the study of citations for measuring and evaluating published materials. This bibliographic tool indexes writings that have made reference to other publications, thus making it possible to determine which writings are cited in later publications and how many times each has been cited by others. Since the *Science citation index* covers publications in a limited number of fields falling into that area commonly called "science and technology," it is of little value for all subject areas that are excluded, such as the humanities. However, such indexes are merely finding devices and the data listed therein are of no value in themselves until they have been culled, sorted, organized and interpreted. Many attempts have been made to study citations and to interpret them in order to find new methodologies for identifying and evaluating writings in a particular subject area.[3]

The study undertaken and detailed herein has been an attempt to find and outline a methodology that could be applied to any subject literature to identify and evaluate significant writings in that field of study.

THE PROBLEM

Many studies have been made using references cited in a specified corpus of writings, and from these investigations have emerged many hypotheses and some notions of what citation analyses can reveal to us about a subject literature, or a specified group of writings. No studies have been sufficiently extensive to enable us to have conclusive proof as to exactly what citation studies actually can offer us and how reliable they might be. But, as more studies are undertaken and completed, it is hoped that in the future some definite facts and conclusions may be stated. This author trusts that his inquiry will develop information that might serve as a contributing factor towards supplying some assertive statements about a subject literature.

The purpose of this investigation is to determine whether the citation relationships connecting the writings that make up a subject literature will point out the significant contributions in that particular field of study. It is therefore hypothesized that there exists a definite network among the citations in a given subject literature that encompasses all the impressive contributions to that field, and that their impact on that subject can be ranked according to the number of times that the same work appears in the overall network. If this network does indeed indicate which are the influential contributions to a subject literature, then there has been established an algorithm for determining which are the most mentioned writings in that subject, on a completely objective basis without personal regard as to their merit.

There is another aspect that should be considered in discussing citation networks. Robert A. Fairthorne has argued in favor of using similar methods to produce what he calls "bibliographical world lines" or "fans" of ancestors for each work.[4] Fairthorne was primarily concerned with making a classification scheme rather than discovering a core literature or the various aspects of a specific subject literature. This study shows that his ideas are valid; it is possible to make a classification scheme from the fan-like network of citations originating from a single work. If several such fans were joined, a broader and stronger classification would emerge. However, to accomplish this would require that a great number of studies like this be done.

PROCEDURE

Unlike previous citation studies, this investigation begins by selecting a single publication from which to start tracing a network, rather than using the citations found in a specified corpus of writings.

The first step was to define the subject area very explicitly, and then to choose a work[5] which fell into that subject. The work chosen should be one that is a history or a review publication of the type usually referred to as a "state of the art report." The publication date of this initial work was of utmost importance since it was used to establish one of the inclusive dates of the materials that were to comprise the network. The other date could have been left open or set, according to the purpose of the study and/or the nature of the subject. In this case a date was set, the details of which are given below. In selecting an appropriate publication it was necessary to ascertain that it contained at least one citation from which tracing and constructing the network of writings could begin. (See Chapter II for the definition of the term "writing.")

Next it was necessary to record the references given in the work chosen as the source publication. From this point on, each new and distinct writing cited was consulted and in turn its references were also noted. Each consultation and recording of items was a step backward in time. Once a writing was consulted and its references taken down, then it was only necessary to keep a tally as to how many times there were references to that particular writing. Its citations had already been recorded for consultation purposes. In this type of experiment the network should increase and fan out almost exponentially, and a careful system had to be devised to record and organize the data collected. Fairthorne described this fanning out very well in his paper on classification, in which he discusses various methods used to "determine membership in a class."[6] He states:

> Bibliographic methods are of course used widely, but often embedded in the "understanding of the subject matter" used as a supposed short cut. Too often it is a detour through irrelevancies, leading to individual conclusions not reached by others. The purely bibliographical methods, necessarily more consistent, include consideration of authors' names, citations, circumstances of production, vocabulary and style. The last two are used, as are others, extra-textually for relation to and comparison with the corpus of discourses.
>
> Whatever characteristics may be used, they are used for one purpose only; to link documents (or records of any kind of any kind of discourse) with documents previously studied. For documents that mention the same things, but are on different topics, will have different ancestors, in the sense of preceding documents to which they are linked by various bibliographic characteristics. Similarly they will have different descendents. So the problem of classifying, not the documents, but the sets of documents that form their histories, bibliographical 'world lines.'
>
> Take, as a simple example, the very strong forms of linkage by direct citation. Texts that mention the same things may cite different earlier documents. These may cite others, earlier than they, and so on. This produces 'fans' or 'spreads' (in the Brouwerian sense) of ancestors that have converged on the documents under consideration.[7]

To accurately construct this "fan" or "spread" and keep it under control at all times, each new item was recorded in duplicate, one copy for a control file and the other copy to be used in the actual search for the item; thus the control file was always complete and up-to-the-minute. The information needed for recording was complete bibliographic information as given in the citation, as well as data on the precise point where it could be verified if need should arise at a later time.

When tracing citations, references will lead to writings which cite no other publications, or to others which refer to works which are out of the scope of the investigation either by reason of time or subject. An end is reached when all references have been consulted and the last work consulted led to no new or relevant citations. With the last consultation the network is completed. At this point the investigator begins to analyze and interpret the data which has been gathered.

The technique just described lends itself readily to the study of a subject literature. Rawski has defined a subject literature as "the available knowledge records pertaining to a subject."[8] The subject literature studied in this investigation was that of "cataloging." This term is defined for the purpose of this study as the process of recording specific bibliographic data about a knowledge record, and the formation of an index or file for this information which will provide easy access to the data contained in it. Aspects of this area of specialization which are specifically included are: determination of author and title entries; descriptive cataloging; the catalog, its formation, use and maintenance; organization and administration of the cataloging department; cost of cataloging; the teaching of cataloging; history of cataloging; and general works. Topics which could be considered as a part of cataloging but which have been definitely excluded from this study are: subject cataloging; filing rules; card reproduction; union catalogs; classified catalogs; shelf lists; centralized and cooperative cataloging; and all aspects of classification.

With this explicit definition of the subject in mind the most appropriate publication with which to begin the network was James Tait's *Authors and titles*, published in 1969.[9] It contains 63 references to previous publications. The dates of the works that comprise this study were established as follows: the choice of Tait's book set the final date at the year 1969. A look into the history of cataloging helped establish the other date. The first cataloging code was that of the British Museum for which Sir Anthony Panizzi was mainly responsible. This code first appeared in 1841, and as it is known that it took several years to complete these cataloging rules, the year 1835 seemed to be a reasonable choice for the other date. This would enable the study to encompass any possible earlier writings that might have influenced or led to the formation of this archetype of cataloging codes. Therefore, the inclusive dates of writings in this analysis are 1835 to 1969, a period of 135 years.

The authors of the works which formulate this network were also studied to ascertain the extent of personal relationships which might have influenced their thoughts in the professional literature. This type of study is referred to as "prosopography" (quantitative collective biography) and is defined by Lawrence Stone:

> Prosopography is the investigation of the common background characteristics of a group of actors in history by means of a collective study of their lives. The method employed is to establish a universe to be studied, and then to ask a set of uniform questions. . . . The various types of information about the individuals in the universe are then juxtaposed and combined, and are examined for significant variables.[10]

The set of uniform questions used in this study concerned the country of residence, education, years at each employing institution, offices held, and so on.

SUMMARY

In brief, each of the 63 writings cited by Tait was traced to see which earlier writings were cited by it. Each consultation of a new writing was a step backward in time, so that as noted above, the network gradually expanded and resembled a fan or a genealogical tree. Those writings which contained no references to earlier works may be said to contain original ideas, at least theoretically, assuming that each author cites his debts to predecessors, a factor not always present. The writings which do acknowledge previous writings and use them as authorities by citing them, may be said to be "offspring" of those earlier writings and the "genes" in the form of ideas should be evident in the later writing. Thus when the network is finished there should be chains of successive generations which share some of the same ideas or should, at least, have been influenced by the prior author's thoughts. The more times that a single work or an author is cited should indicate how strong its influence has been in comparison with others. Garfield expressed these same thoughts by saying:

> High citation counts reflect impact but may not reflect intrinsic worth. The data obtained from citation analysis are always relative rather than absolute.[11]

Thus, in theory, an author who is cited once cannot be said to have been as inspiring (for better or for worse) as one who was cited by many different authors at various periods in time.

FOOTNOTES

1. See Appendix III for a list of previous studies of citation use and analysis.
2. *Science citation index; an international interdisciplinary index to the literature of science*. Philadelphia, Institute for Scientific Information, 1961— .
3. Price, Derek J. D. "Networks of scientific paper," *Science*, 149: 510-515, July 30, 1965.
   Westbrook, J. H. "Identifying significant research," *Science*, 132: 1229-1234, October 28, 1960.
   Lehnus, Donald J. "JEL, 1960-1970; an analytical study," *Journal of education for librarianship*, 12:71-83, Fall, 1971.
   Lehnus, Donald J. "Who cited what? A citation analysis of the four basic cataloging texts," *Journal of the American Society for Information Science*, 23:100-108, March-April 1972.
   Velke, Lissa. "The use of citation patterns in the identification of 'research front' authors and 'classic' papers." In: American Society for Information Science. *The information conscious society; proceedings of the 33rd annual meeting of ASIS*, Washington, 1970, pp. 49-51.
4. Fairthorne, Robert A., "Temporal structure in bibliographical classification," paper read at the Ottawa Conference on the Conceptual Classification of Knowledge, Ottawa University, October 4, 1971.
5. For definitions of the terms "work" and "writing" see Chapter II.
6. Fairthorne, Robert A. "Temporal structure in bibliographical classification," p. 10.
7. *Ibid.*, pp. 10-11.
8. Rawski, Conrad. "Subject literatures and librarianship." In: Bone, Larry Earl. *Library school teaching methods; courses in the selection of adult materials*, Urbana, Univ. of Illinois, 1969. p. 97.

9. Tait, James Adie. *Authors and titles; an analytical study of the author concept in codes of cataloguing rules in the English language, from that of the British Museum in 1841 to the Anglo-American cataloguing rules 1967.* Hamden, Conn., Archon Books, 1969. 154p.

10. Stone, Lawrence. "Prosopography," *Daedalus*, Winter, 1971. p. 46.

11. Garfield, Eugene. *The use of citation data in writing the history of science.* Philadelphia, Institute for Scientific Information, 1964. p. 1.

CHAPTER II

THE RAW MATERIAL OF THE STUDY: DEFINITIONS AND PARAMETERS

This entire study is dependent on "citations" as found in "works" and "writings," and it is imperative that it be made perfectly clear what has been meant by a "writing" and a "work," and what has been considered as a "citation."

WHAT IS A WRITING? WHAT IS A WORK?

The use of the word "writing" throughout this study indicates an item that can be considered unique bibliographically. It is used here as a synonym for what Lubetzky and Hayes term "book."[1] *Book* usually implies a separately published monographic text, and for this reason "writing" is used in order to include such terms as periodical articles and individual contributions which may form part of another publication or appear in a collection. The term "work" refers collectively to all editions, versions, and translations of a specific text. The terms "book" (i.e., "writing") and "work" have been used according to the definitions of Lubetzky and Hayes in their discussion of physical records wherein they distinguish them by saying:

> The essence of the modern concept of cataloging, which might more appropriately be called "bibliographic cataloging," has gradually emerged from a growing realization of the fact that the *book* (i.e., the material record) and the *work* (i.e., the intellectual product embodied in it) are not coterminous; that, in cataloging, the *medium* is not the message; that the *book* is actually only one representation of a certain work which may be found in a given library or system of libraries in different media (books, manuscripts, films, phonorecords, punched and magnetic tapes, braille), different forms (editions, translations, versions), and even under different titles; . . . .[2]

"Edition" is used here to mean that there are changes in the text, and not merely a reprinting of the text. If the text is the same, but with a different imprint it is considered the same edition. Such is often the case when books are published simultaneously by American and British publishers. Also, it is not uncommon to find the same writing appearing in two different publications, e.g., an article that was later published in another periodical or in an anthology; again, this would be considered as one "writing." If an article in English were translated into French and published in a French periodical it would be considered as a distinct "writing" but the same "work." A major change has taken place in its format, but its text is (or should be) intact.

A "new" edition should indicate that changes, updating and/or corrections have altered the text. This, in turn, ought to indicate the addition of new citations, and possibly the deletion of previous ones, even though many would probably remain the same as in the older edition. For this reason, each edition or translation of a work referred to was considered as a different publication in tracing and constructing the network. At this point the study deviates from the Lubetzky-Hayes "work," but in the final analysis of the most frequently cited literature all editions, versions and translations were considered as a single "work."

Publications containing the output of two or more persons were perused and analyzed, and in cases where the writing of each author could be separated and distinguished as individual contributions, the parts were counted as separate publications, but a publication written jointly without such distinction was considered as a single writing. When a collection or anthology containing several separable and distinguishable writings was referred to in its entirety, each writing contained therein was treated as though it were cited individually. The reason for this was that quite often one of those writings was cited by someone without making reference to the whole collection or anthology. Such was the case with those papers contained in Mary Piggott's collection of lectures given at the University of London School of Librarianship.[3] Another example is the Medical Library Association's *Handbook* containing a chapter on cataloging. In the first edition (1943)[4] this chapter was written by Laura Marguerite Prime, but in the second edition (1956)[5] the author was Wilma Troxell. Each of these librarians was credited with a citation according to which edition of the *Handbook* was cited, as well as when the author was referred to by name.

Personal correspondence, annual reports, intra-office memos, and other similar unpublished materials were not recorded and do not figure in the network. This decision is based on the fact that this type of material is extremely difficult, if at all possible, to obtain, and the probabilities of containing references are very minimal. Also, materials which had such a limited availability probably could not have made a great impact on the subject literature as a whole.

Language was not a limiting factor; all references that fell into the scope of this investigation were included in the network regardless of the language in which they were written.

WHAT IS A CITATION?

The words "citation" and "reference" are commonly used interchangeably, but in actuality there is a subtle difference. Webster's Unabridged[6] defines the two terms thusly:

> Citation—Act of citing a passage from a book in its own words, or from another person; also, the passage or words cited; quotations; . . . .[7]

> Reference—A specific direction of the attention; a sign or direction referring a reader to another passage or book.[8]

Price has suggested that these terms not be used interchangeably and he proposes and adopts:

> ... the convention that if Paper R contains a bibliographic footnote using and describing Paper C, the R contains a reference to C, and C has a citation from R. The number of references a paper has is measured by the number of items in its bibliography as endnotes and footnotes, etc. while the number of citations a paper has is found by looking it up in some sort of citation index and seeing how many other papers mention it.[9]

For uniformity and clarity Price's definitions of these nouns are adhered to in this paper. But, the verb forms, "to cite" and "to refer" have been used synonymously. Webster's definitions are:

> Cite—To quote, as a passage from a book, usually by way of authority or proof.[10]

> Refer—To send or direct (to some person or place), as for treatment, aid, information, decision, etc.[11]

There are many reasons for referring to other writings and it would be a laborious task to attempt to ascertain the reasons for each reference included by an author. However, Ben-Ami Lipetz attempted to analyze relationships between the citing paper and its references.[12]

Another person who has studied and written about citations and citation indexing is Melvin Weintraub, who states that:

> Citation indexing is based on the simple concept that an author's references to previously recorded information identify much of the earlier work that is pertinent to the subject of his present document.[13]

If this be true, then the network of citations which was proposed and outlined earlier will be made up of all the earlier works that are pertinent to the subject of James Tait's *Authors and titles*, that is, cataloging. The appearance of any writing in the network will then only indicate that it is somehow related to this subject. It will not point out if it is a weak or a strong relationship, or the importance of that writing.

Weintraub also attempted to give a list of reasons why authors cite other works and writings. In discussing the reference tradition he says:

> Scientific tradition requires that when a reputable scientist or technologist publishes an article, he should refer to earlier articles which relate to his theme. These references are supposed to identify those earlier researchers whose concepts, methods, apparatus, etc., inspired or were used by the author in developing his own article. Some specific reasons for using citations are as follows:
>
> 1. Paying homage to pioneers.
> 2. Giving credit for related work.

3. Identifying methodology, equipment, etc.
4. Providing background reading.
5. Correcting one's own work.
6. Correcting the work of others.
7. Criticizing previous work.
8. Substantiating claims.
9. Alerting researchers to forthcoming work.
10. Providing leads to poorly disseminated, poorly indexed, or uncited work.
11. Authenticating data and classes of fact—physical constants, etc.
12. Identifying original publications in which an idea or concept was discussed.
13. Identifying the original publication describing an eponymic concept or term as, e.g., Hodgkin's Disease, Pareto's Law, Friedel-Crafts Reaction.
14. Disclaiming work or ideas of others.
15. Disputing priority claims of others.[17]

As it is not possible to determine an author's reasons for listing all of his references to other writings, the investigation being detailed here is based on cited works regardless of whether the author's *intention* was to refute the work of someone else or to substantiate his own work.

References are not always easy to identify or to find. They may appear anywhere in a writing: in the preliminary pages, buried in the text, in footnotes throughout the text, or listed in a group somewhere towards the back of the publication. When they appear at the end of the text they are often under such headings as "references," "notes," "bibliography," "literature consulted," "acknowledgements," or any other similar wording. Those given in footnotes should also appear in the list at the end, but whether they do or not depends on the whim of the author. Often it is quite difficult to interpret such headings as "readings" or "further readings" without studying the publications listed and attempting to determine the author's reasons for their inclusion. It is not uncommon to find at the end of a writing two lists of publications, one containing publications actually used, and the other a list of writings which the author is suggesting for further reading on a topic, or just simply to give a list of published materials for one reason or another. Mere lists of writings given for the sole purpose of offering a list of readings on a particular topic, or any other similar reason for including a "bibliography" *per se* have not been considered as citations for the purpose of this investigation.

In any given writing one might find that there are works mentioned which are not "references" *per se*, but rather are referred to as examples of topography, problems of cataloging, or for any other such reason which in no way is concerned with the intellectual content of the works, but rather with their physical properties. While in the process of analyzing a list of "notes," "bibliography" or whatever the heading may be, one immediately recognizes that these lists often contain what are virtually "annotated footnotes," that is, commentary or additional information supplied by the author with no reference to any other publications. This type of note is frequently intercalated in the list of references.

Due to the broad scope of this undertaking, it has been impossible to read the entire text of each publication included in the network, but every page of each cited writing has been scanned for quotations, footnotes, bibliographies, and every other form in which an author may have referred to some other writing. The text of the preface, introduction and any other writing in the preliminary pages were all read in case they might contain other cited materials.

References to other works are sometimes footnoted by editors. This type of reference not made by the author has been disregarded.

SUMMARY

As used in this study a "writing" is an item which can be considered unique bibliographically and may be a monograph, a journal article or any contribution to a larger publication, such as an anthology or a festschrift; "work" is a term used to encompass all editions, versions and translations of a specific text. The entire text of each item was searched for "references" made to specific works. "Lists of readings," "notes," and "bibliographies" were perused to determine which were references included by the author to give credit for their intellectual content and which were merely suggested readings or annotated footnotes.

FOOTNOTES

1. Lubetzky, Seymour, and R. M. Hayes. "Bibliographic dimensions in information control," *American documentation*, 20:247-252, July 1969.
2. *Ibid.*, p. 248.
3. Piggott, Mary. *Cataloguing principles and practice; an inquiry.* London, The Library Association, 1954. 159p.
4. Medical Library Association. *Handbook of medical library practice.* Chicago, 1943. 609p.
5. Medical Library Association. *Handbook of medical library practice.* 2d ed. Chicago, 1956. 601p.
6. *Webster's new international dictionary of the English language.* 2d ed. unabridged. Springfield, Mass., Merriam Co., 1949. 3210p.
7. *Ibid.*, p. 491.
8. *Ibid.*, p. 2092.
9. Price, Derek. "Citation measures of hard science, soft science, technology, and nonscience," In: Nelson, Carnot E. and Donald K. Pollack. *Communication among scientists and engineers.* Lexington, Mass., D. C. Heath, 1970. p. 7.
10. *Webster's new international dictionary of the English language.* p. 491.
11. *Ibid.*, p. 2091.

12. Lipetz, Ben-Ami. *The feasibility of improving future citation indexes; a progress report.* New York, American Institute of Physics, 1964. (Report AIP/DRP-C2, 1964.) 7p.
13. Weintraub, Melvin. "Citation indexes," In: *Encyclopedia of library and information science.* New York, Marcel Dekker, 1971. Vol. 5, p. 16.
14. *Ibid.*, p. 19.

CHAPTER III

AN OVERVIEW OF THE TOTAL CONSTRUCTED NETWORK

The examination of all the 63 references made by Tait in his *Authors and titles* and their analysis according to the definitions established in the preceding chapter resulted in a total of 71 references to earlier writings with which to proceed in building the network. These references covered a diversity of subjects. Thus the network began to spread out in many directions. By tracing further references the network was developed and began to grow exponentially.

When fully completed the entire network contained a total of 7,209 citations of 2,532 works. There were 76 references to writings which were unidentifiable or unverifiable and 21 references to writings which were identified and verified but were unobtainable. Thus there were only 97 writings which could not be consulted to add their references to the network. However, these 97 writings amount to less than 4 percent (21 unobtainable writings are 0.83 percent and the 76 unidentifiable are 3 percent) of the total 2,532 works that make up the network.

These 2,532 works were written by a total of 1,412 personal and corporate authors, including joint authors.

THE MOST CITED AUTHORS

Table 1 lists 86 authors who were cited at least 15 times. At the right of each name is a number indicating the total times that author's writings appeared in the network. The asterisk which follows some of the names indicates those who were cited at least 15 times, but had no single work which was cited as many as 8 times. Table 2 lists the number of authors according to how many times each was cited in the network.

The 86 authors in Table 1 represent 6.7 percent of the 1,412 authors which comprise the network and were responsible for 3,614 (50.12 percent) of the total of 7,209 citations. This number is slightly less than the total citations (3,892) in Table 1 because it is necessary to discount those which were written by joint authors.

Appendix II lists 141 authors whose works were the most frequently cited. Of the 141 *authors*, 125 are personal and 16 are corporate authors. A concentrated effort was made to furnish complete names and dates for each of these 125 personal authors. Some dates were impossible to locate, and for those authors for whom neither a birth nor a death date could be ascertained, "flourished" dates are given to show when they began to publish.

TABLE 1

Authors Cited 15 or More Times in the Network

	Author	Total Citations in Network
1.	American Library Association	332
2.	Lubetzky, Seymour	189
3.	Cutter, Charles A.	181
4.	Osborn, Andrew D.	118
5.	The Library Association	113
6.	Library of Congress	110
7.	Mann, Margaret	107
8.	Hanson, James C. M.	104
9.	Tauber, Maurice F.	104
10.	Ranganathan, S. R.	100
11.	Wright, Wyllis E.	83
12.	Bishop, William Warner	78
13.	Sharp, Henry Alexander	62
14.	Akers, Susan Grey	61
15.	Rider, A. Fremont	60
16.	British Museum	59
17.	Brown, James Duff	55
18.	Jewett, Charles C.	52
19.	Dewey, Melvil	51
20.	Vatican Library	49
21.	Metcalf, Keyes DeWitt*	48
22.	Taube, Mortimer	47
23.	Quinn, John Henry	46
24.	Hitchler, Theresa	45
25.	Fellows, Jennie Dorcas	44
26.	Haskins, Susan	44
27.	Nyholm, Amy F. Wood	44
28.	Pettee, Julia	43
29.	Sayers, W. C. Berwick	43
30.	Currier, T. Franklin	42
31.	Stewart, James D.	41
32.	Miller, Robert A.	39
33.	Morsch, Lucile M.*	39
34.	Jolley, Leonard J.	38
35.	Prussian instructions	38
36.	Pierson, Harriet W.	37

*These authors had no single work which was cited as many as eight times.

TABLE 1—Cont'd

	Author	Total Citations in Network
37.	Chaplin, Arthur Hugh	35
38.	Kaiser, Rudolf	34
39.	MacPherson, Harriet D.	34
40.	Fletcher, William Isaac	33
41.	Trotier, Arnold H.*	33
42.	Dean, Hazel	30
43.	Swank, Raynard Coe	30
44.	Wheatley, Henry B.	30
45.	Dunkin, Paul S.	29
46.	International Federation of Library Associations	28
47.	Ellsworth, Ralph E.	27
48.	Randall, William Madison	27
49.	Jast, Louis Stanley*	26
50.	Ellinger, Werner Bruno	25
51.	Bodleian Library	24
52.	Institute on Catalog Code Revision	24
53.	Linderfelt, Klas A.	24
54.	Mudge, Isadore Gilbert	24
55.	Verona, Eva	24
56.	Delisle, Leopold	23
57.	Graesel, Arnim	23
58.	Coney, Donald	22
59.	MacDonald, M. Ruth*	22
60.	Wallace, Ruth	22
61.	Wilson, Louis Round	21
62.	Henkle, Herman H.	20
63.	Italy. Direzione generale delle accademie e biblioteche	20
64.	Childs, James Bennett	19
65.	Josephson, Aksel G. S.	19
66.	Berthold, Arthur B.	18
67.	Bostwick, Arthur E.	18
68.	Dziatzko, Karl	18
69.	Gjelsness, Rudolph H.*	18
70.	Gull, Cloyd Dake	18
71.	Kingery, Robert E.*	18
72.	Martel, Charles	18
73.	Spalding, Charles Sumner*	18
74.	Ver Nooy, Winifred	18
75.	Frels, Wilhelm	17
76.	MacNair, Mary Wilson	17
77.	Wells, Arthur James	17
78.	Allez, George Clare	16

TABLE 1—Cont'd

	Author	Total Citations in Network
79.	Lane, William Coolidge*	16
80.	Panizzi, Sir Anthony	16
81.	Spain. Junta Técnica de Archivos, Bibliotecas y Museos	16
82.	Strout, Ruth French	16
83.	Custer, Benjamin	15
84.	Fuchs, Hermann	15
85.	Howe, Harriet Emma	15
86.	Norris, Dorothy May	15

TABLE 2

Total Number of Authors and the Number of Times Each was Cited

  86 authors were cited 15 or more times each.*
    7 authors were cited 14 times each.
    7 authors were cited 13 times each.
    9 authors were cited 12 times each.
  25 authors were cited 11 times each.
  19 authors were cited 10 times each.
  16 authors were cited 9 times each.
  25 authors were cited 8 times each.
  20 authors were cited 7 times each.
  39 authors were cited 6 times each.
  49 authors were cited 5 times each.
  79 authors were cited 4 times each.
136 authors were cited 3 times each.
251 authors were cited 2 times each.
644 authors were cited 1 time each.

1412 authors

---

*See Table 1 for the exact number of times that each of these 86 authors was cited.

It should be pointed out that 9 of the 86 authors in Table 1 had no single work which was ever cited eight times. Even though these authors (Rudolph Gjelsness, L. Stanley Jast, Robert Kingery, William C. Lane, Ruth MacDonald, Keyes D. Metcalf, Lucile M. Morsch, C. Sumner Spalding and Arnold Trotier) were frequently cited, they wrote no single work which was *often* cited. For this reason Appendix II is divided into two parts: Part A— Authors of works which were cited eight or more times, and Part B— Frequently cited authors which had no single work cited as many as eight times.

THE MOST CITED WORKS

During the construction of the network each citation was arranged alphabetically by author or main entry, and subarranged by title. Thus when the network was completed it was only necessary to study the citations of any given author and ascertain which writings were versions, translations or editions of the same works. All works which had been referred to at least eight times were pulled and a new file of "most cited works" was created. There resulted a total of 184 *works* by 132 authors (including joint authors) which had been cited at least eight times. These 184 *works* are given in Appendix I with full bibliographic detail.

Each of the 184 *works* was studied and classified according to topic or aspect of cataloging treated therein. There resulted 15 categories into which all the works could be classified. The following definitions explain and give the scope of each category.

1. Cataloging codes—The actual codes of rules, and not writings about them.
2. Development of codes—Overall views on code revision; the effects of changes on library catalogs; problems resulting from a revision as well as problems involved in the process of developing a new code.
3. Cataloging manuals—The how-to-do-it books; these often serve as texts in basic cataloging courses.
4. Theory—Writings which are for the most part theoretical and deal with the principles of authorship and cataloging in general.
5. History—The history of cataloging, cataloging codes, and the comparison of various codes.
6. Corporate entry—Theory, history and development of corporate entries in cataloging.
7. Descriptive cataloging—The description of an item with the purpose of distinguishing it from other items, expressly excluding the choice and determination of the form of main and secondary headings.
8. Selective cataloging—Also referred to as "economies in cataloging"; the elimination of superfluous and excessive detail, and

overelaboration in the process of cataloging; the cataloging of an item according to the needs of a particular library or of the specific item in hand.
9. Cataloging in special situations—Differences in cataloging according to the needs of various classes of users; problems of recataloging.
10. Special materials—Guides and procedures for the cataloging of maps and atlases; serials and periodicals; and music.
11. Catalogs—The formation, use and maintenance of library catalogs.
12. Divided catalogs—The division of library catalogs into either author-title and subject catalogs, or the three-way division of authors, subjects and titles.
13. Administration—The organization and management of technical services.
14. Cost of cataloging—The analysis and determination of the cost of technical services, and cost accounting for libraries.
15. Bibliography and library science—This is the catch-all category to include general works on libraries and library science with sections dealing in some way with cataloging, and works on general bibliography.

Table 3 lists these 15 categories and shows the number of works classed into each group and the percentage of the 184 works that fall into that category. Also shown are the number of citations made for each class and the percentage of the total citations made for the 184 most cited works.

SUMMARY

Thus it can be seen that the network emerged and extended into all aspects of cataloging as defined in Chapter I. Tait's *Authors and titles* served very well as a key to opening up the network and discovering the connections that led into all of the 2,532 works and their 1,412 authors. From this, a core literature based on frequency of citation was easily obtained.

When the 184 most cited works were grouped according to their similarities they created a small classification scheme consisting of the 15 categories just described, which range from the very general to the specific. This verified Fairthorne's suggestion that a classification may be made from the "bibliographical world lines" created by one or more works, and in this case it was done by using a single work.

A number of conclusions can be drawn from the foregoing tables. An analysis of Table 1 points out that less than 7 percent of the authors wrote over 50 percent of the writings cited. The titles in the categories of "cataloging codes" and "cataloging manuals" were cited much more heavily than the average. Of the 184 works the average title was cited about 16 times, but the cataloging codes and manuals were each cited an average of 28 times. Even though the codes and manuals make up only 21 percent of the works cited,

TABLE 3

Subject Analysis of the Most Frequently Cited Works

	Subjects	Number of Works		Number of Citations	
1.	Cataloging codes	24	(13.0%)	684	(23.5%)
2.	Development of codes	12	(06.5%)	131	(04.5%)
3.	Cataloging manuals	15	(08.0%)	422	(14.5%)
4.	Theory	13	(07.0%)	224	(07.5%)
5.	History	15	(08.0%)	188	(06.5%)
6.	Corporate entry	12	(06.5%)	151	(05.0%)
7.	Descriptive cataloging	5	(03.0%)	75	(02.5%)
8.	Selective cataloging	9	(05.0%)	121	(04.0%)
9.	Cataloging in special situations	8	(04.0%)	90	(03.0%)
10.	Special materials	7	(04.0%)	89	(03.0%)
11.	Catalogs	20	(11.0%)	241	(08.0%)
12.	Divided catalogs	11	(06.0%)	142	(05.0%)
13.	Administration	7	(04.0%)	77	(03.0%)
14.	Cost of cataloging	11	(06.0%)	116	(04.0%)
15.	Bibliography and library science	15	(08.0%)	166	(06.0%)
	Totals	184	(100.0%)	2917	(100.0%)

they account for 38 percent of the citations in the network. The percentage of works cited and the number of citations for the other thirteen categories are almost equal. From this it may be seen that the codes and manuals are much more often referred to than materials of the other categories.

CHAPTER IV

ANALYSIS OF THE MOST FREQUENTLY CITED WORKS AND THEIR AUTHORS

THE AUTHORS

The complete names and dates of the 132 authors of the 184 most often cited works are listed in Part A of Appendix II. The list contains 16 corporate authors, 34 women, and 82 men. Table 4 shows the number of works corresponding to each of these categories. It should be noted that the number of works produced by corporate authors is in direct proportion to their percentage of the total number of authors. On the other hand, women account for a lesser number of works than their total number would indicate. The 82 men were slightly more productive per capita than were the women.

TABLE 4

Categories of Authors and Their Production

Authors	Total Number		Number of Works Produced	
Men	82	(61.5%)	120	(65.25%)
Women	34	(26.5%)	41	(22.25%)
Corporate bodies	16	(12.0%)	23	(12.50%)
Totals	132	(100.0%) Authors	184	(100.00%) Works

Some interesting details may be found concerning these authors. Table 5 analyzes their nationality and productivity. Birthplace was not considered, but rather the country in which the person lived and was active professionally. The nationality of corporate authors was determined by the country in which the corporate body is located. The nationalities of the 16 corporate authors are as follows: four American, four British, two Italian, and one each for Denmark, Germany, Norway, Spain, Sweden and an international organization. In this study the authorship of works produced by individuals in connection with a corporate body was attributed to the individual.[1]

TABLE 5

Nationality of the 132 Authors and Their Productivity

Nationality	Number of Authors		Number of Works	
American	82	(62.00%)	124	(67.00%)
British	25	(20.00%)	30	(17.00%)
German	10	(07.25%)	12	(06.50%)
French	5	(04.00%)	5	(02.75%)
Italian	3	(02.25%)	3	(01.75%)
Indian	1	(00.75%)	4	(02.25%)
Danish	1	(00.75%)	1	(00.55%)
Norwegian	1	(00.75%)	1	(00.55%)
Spanish	1	(00.75%)	1	(00.55%)
Swedish	1	(00.75%)	1	(00.55%)
Yugoslav	1	(00.75%)	1	(00.55%)
International organization	1	(00.75%)	1	(00.55%)
Totals	132	(100.00%)	184	(100.00%)

A disproportionate number of the authors were born in the twentieth century. Of the 116 authors, 42 (36%) were born between 1900 and 1915. The year 1915 is the latest in which any of these was born. In the last quarter of the nineteenth century 40 (35%) were born. Between 1850 and 1874, 20 authors (17.5%) were born. Ten (8.5%) were born in the second quarter of the nineteenth century. Only Charles Jewett and Edward Edwards were born in the first quarter of the nineteenth century. There were only two, Anthony Panizzi and Leopold Hesse, who were born in the eighteenth century. For those authors for whom neither birth nor death dates could be established, the birth dates were estimated to have been forty years prior to their first publication.

THE WORKS

The works themselves also yield interesting details. English has distinguished itself as the foremost language in cataloging over the entire 135 year period covered by this study. It is the language in which the majority of the most cited works were written. Only 24 (13%) of the 184 works were not originally published in English. Table 6 lists the languages and the number of works which appeared in each.

TABLE 6

Languages of the Original Publications

Language	Number of Works	Percentage of Total
English	160	87.00%
German	12	6.50%
French	5	2.50%
Italian	3	1.50%
Danish	1	0.625%
Norwegian	1	0.625%
Spanish	1	0.625%
Swedish	1	0.625%
	184	100.00%

It was possible to classify each of the 184 works as one of the following types of publications: (1) monograph, (2) periodical article, or (3) *contribution* to a monograph or conference. Table 7 shows the groups into which the works fall according to the type of publication, and by country in which the original work was published; the United States, Great Britain and other foreign countries.

TABLE 7

Type of Publication and Country of Origin

Type of Publication	Number of Works	United States	Great Britain	Others
Monographs	82 (44%)	45 (24.0%)	16 (8.5%)	21 (11.5%)
Periodical articles	73 (40%)	63 (34.5%)	2 (1.0%)	8 (4.5%)
Contributions to monographs and conference proceedings	29 (16%)	17 (9.5%)	11 (6.0%)	1 (0.5%)
Totals	184 (100%)	125 (68.0%)	29 (15.5%)	30 (16.5%)

MONOGRAPHS

With monographs a division in English language works becomes apparent. Table 8 shows the percentage of works published in the United States, Great Britain and other foreign countries according to the type of publication. In the United States, a much larger proportion of writings appeared in periodicals than was the case in Great Britain and other foreign countries. In Great Britain more than one-half of the most cited works appeared in monographic form, while in the United States more than one-half appeared in periodicals. In non-English speaking countries the percentage of works in monographic form zooms to 70 percent.

PERIODICALS

As shown in Table 7 there were 73 works published in periodicals, mostly American. Surprisingly the three serials devoted principally to cataloging and classification do not seem to have been responsible for publishing a large share of the most cited articles. These three are: (1) *Catalogers' and classifiers' yearbook*, of which there appeared 11 numbers from 1929 to 1945; (2) the *Journal of cataloging and classification*, published quarterly from 1948 to 1956; and (3) *Library resources and technical services*, published quarterly from 1957 to the present. All three are publications of the American Library Association.

TABLE 8
Distribution of Monographs, Articles and
Contributions within the U.S., Great Britain,
and Other Countries

Type of Publication	United States		Great Britain		Others	
Monographs	45	(36.0%)	16	(55%)	21	(70.00%)
Periodical articles	63	(50.4%)	2	(7%)	8	(27.66%)
Contributions to monographs and conference proceedings	17	(13.6%)	11	(38%)	1	(3.34%)
Totals	125	(100.0%)	29	(100%)	30	(100.00%)

No article from *Library resources and technical services* was cited more than seven times. Very likely this is due to the fact that it began publication very late in the period covered by the network. At first glance the *Journal of cataloging and classification* appears to have contributed its fair share to the literature which is frequently cited, but when one looks at the five articles from this journal it becomes apparent that they all were published in the same issue, and all the papers presented at a conference on the Lubetzky report[2] held in Los Angeles in 1953. Besides the five papers presented at that conference, no other article in this journal was cited eight times. The oldest of these three, the *Catalogers' and classifiers' yearbook*, included nine articles which are among the most frequently cited works. It was two *general* library science periodicals, *Library quarterly* and *Library journal*, that published almost one-half of the periodical articles that appeared among the 184 works.

Table 9 lists the periodicals which published the most cited works, also given are the percentages of the 73 articles represented by each periodical and the percentage of the 184 works. Of these 14 journals, there are nine American, two British, one each from Germany and Austria, and one international periodical. It should be noted that the *Library Association record* does not appear in this list, and that not a single article from a French journal was cited enough to be included.

CONTRIBUTIONS TO OTHER PUBLICATIONS

Of the 29 works classed as *contributions* to monographs and conference proceedings, 21 are obtainable in just three publications of collected works. These three collections are:

1. Institute on Cataloging Code Revision, Stanford University, 1958. *Working papers*. Stanford, Calif., 1958. 1 vol.
2. Piggott, Mary, editor. *Cataloguing principles and practice; an inquiry*. London, The Library Association, 1954. 159p.
3. Randall, William Madison, editor. *The acquisition and cataloging of books*. Chicago, University of Chicago Press, 1940. 408p.

PUBLISHERS

An analysis of the publishers of the most cited works was made to determine if there was any particular type of publisher, such as a library organization, government or university press, which was responsible for publications dealing with cataloging. There is quite an assortment to be found in the publishers of the 184 works, but only three are outstanding. These three, the American Library Association, the University of Chicago, and the United States Government Printing Office, are responsible for 82 (44.5%) of the 184 most cited works. Table 10 lists publishers as a whole with special attention to these three publishers.

TABLE 9
Periodicals Which Published Articles on Cataloging

Periodical	Number of Articles	Percentage of the 73 Articles	Percentage of the 184 Works
Library quarterly	22	30.00%	12.00%
Library journal	13	18.00%	7.00%
Catalogers' and classifiers' yearbook	9	12.25%	5.00%
College and research libraries	6	8.25%	3.25%
Journal of cataloging and classification	5	7.00%	2.75%
Library trends	4	5.50%	2.25%
Zentralblatt für Bibliothekswesen	4	5.50%	2.25%
Libri	2	2.70%	1.10%
PNLA quarterly	2	2.70%	1.10%
Zeitschrift für Bibliothekswesen und Bibliographie	2	2.70%	1.10%
Dartmouth College Library bulletin	1	1.35%	0.55%
Journal of documentation	1	1.35%	0.55%
Librarian and book world	1	1.35%	0.55%
Wilson bulletin	1	1.35%	0.55%
Total	73	100.00%	40.00%

TABLE 10

Publishers of the Most Cited Works

Publisher	Number of Works	Percentage of Total	Monographs	Articles	Contributions
American Library Association	41	22.25%	14	20	7
University of Chicago	33	17.90%	4	22	7
Government Printing Office (including the Library of Congress)	14	7.60%	13	0	1
Subtotals	88	47.75%	31	42	9
Commercial publishers	53	28.80%	33	19	1
Library associations (except A.L.A.)	22	11.90%	5	7	10
Other types of associations	3	1.65%	1	0	2
Libraries (except Library of Congress)	12	6.60%	11	0	1
Universities (except University of Chicago)	6	3.30%	1	5	0
Subtotals	96	52.25%	51	31	14
Totals	184	100.00%	82	73	29

PUBLICATION DATES

The most informative of all these tables is Table 11 covering the dates of publication. The entire 135 year period (1835-1969) used in this study is well represented in the publication dates of the 184 works. Table 11 is a graph illustrating the broad spectrum and points out the most productive eras. For obvious reasons, the date used in this graph for a publication which has appeared in various editions and/or versions is that of the first edition.

Appreciation of the value of the information yielded by Table 11 requires some acquaintance with the history of cataloging during the 135 year period covered. This graph begins with the era in which Panizzi produced the rules for the British Museum. The initial period is then followed by the work of Jewett. Tait commented in his history of cataloging codes: "After the publication of the British Museum rules in 1841, the initiative passed to the other side of the Atlantic, and rested...."[3] The Civil War intervened, Jewett died, and in 1876 Cutter emerged. From that date on the output increases steadily.

Two very fertile periods are immediately apparent—the decades of the 1930's and the 1950's. During the 1930's, 37 (20%) of the 184 works were published, and in the 1950's, 50 (27%) of the most cited works appeared. Even the drop in the 1940's never went below the peak of the 1920's.

During the decade, 1930-1939, the Division of Cataloging and Classification of the American Library Association was quite active. The A.L.A. Committee on Catalog Code Revision was organized in 1932 and was responsible for the publication of the preliminary edition of the new code in 1941. The Depression made catalogers study seriously the costs of cataloging and forced them to give much attention to "selective cataloging." It was during this period that the first serial publication exclusively for cataloging and classification made its appearance, and reached its heyday.

In 1953 Lubetzky published his criticism of the A.L.A. cataloging code.[4] This forceful and logical exposition was the catalyst for much serious and often heated discussion, and marked the beginning of a thorough analysis of cataloging codes. Eventually all this activity resulted in the publication of a new code in 1967.[5] Continuous code revision is still going on at the present and another code is projected for early publication.

SUMMARY

Since the publication of Jewett's proposals for stereotyping catalogs by separate titles and his cataloging rules in 1852 the United States has been the leader in the field of cataloging. This is verified by the large percentage of oft-cited works which were written by Americans. It is interesting to note that of the 116 personal authors, 78 are American, 21 British, 9 German, and 5 are French; also there is one each from Italy (Giuseppe Fumagalli), India (S. R. Ranganathan), and Yugoslavia (Eva Verona). The percentage of Americans and British in this group has made English the most important language in this field. Table 6 points out that 160 (87%) of these most cited works were written in English.

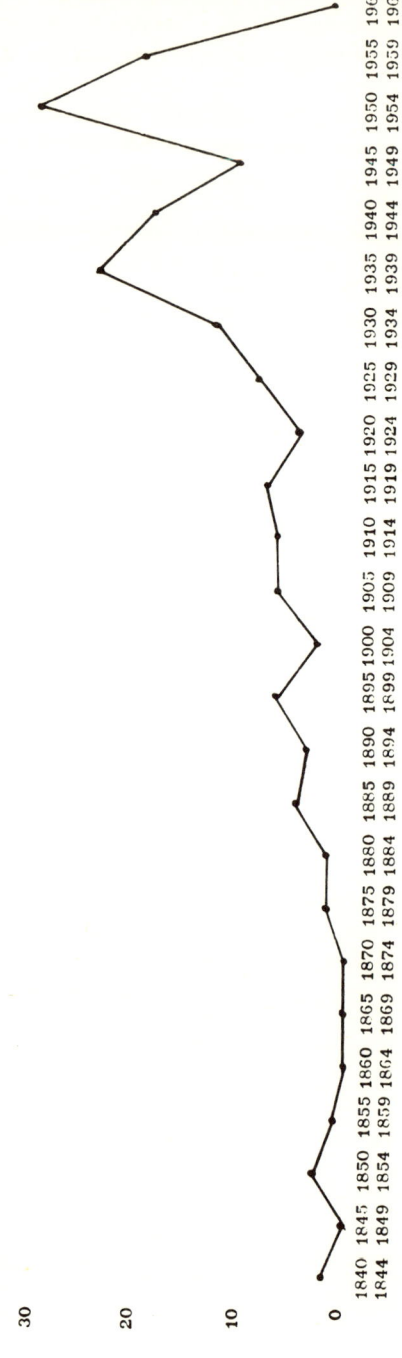

TABLE 11—Publication Dates of the Most Cited Works

Men not only wrote more of the most cited works than did women, but also the number of writings per capita was higher for men than for women. But, it should be noted that of the 34 women authors, 30 (88%) are Americans; 3 are British and 1 is Yugoslav.

As the world leader in cataloging the United States also pioneered and led in the use of periodicals for disseminating writings in cataloging. Everywhere else the monograph was used more extensively than the article. The importance of American periodicals in this field is shown in Table 9 which points out that six American periodicals published 59 (32.25%) of the 184 works.

Table 11 clearly brings out the high production rate of the 1930's and 1950's. The period 1930 to 1959 saw the publication of 117 (63%) of the most frequently cited works. In direct relation to this, it was pointed out that 82 (71%) of the 116 authors were born in the 40 year period, 1875 to 1915; the majority of these would be in their professional prime during the 30 year period 1930 to 1959.

As might be expected, the American Library Association is the largest single publisher of the most cited works, but the University of Chicago ranks second. These two have been responsible for the publication of 74 (40.15%) of the most cited works in cataloging.

FOOTNOTES

1. E.g., Henkle, Herman Henry. *Studies of descriptive cataloging; a report to the Librarian of Congress by the Director of the Processing Department.* Washington, Govt. Print. Off., 1946. 48p.
2. Lubetzky, Seymour. *Cataloging rules and principles; a critique of the A.L.A. rules for entry and a proposed design for their revision.* Washington, Govt. Print. Off., 1953. 65p.
3. Tait, James. *Authors and titles.* p. 31.
4. Lubetzky, Seymour. *Cataloging rules and principles.*
5. *Anglo-American cataloging rules.* Chicago, American Library Association, 1967. 400p.

CHAPTER V

INTERRELATIONSHIPS AMONG THE MOST CITED AUTHORS: INDIVIDUALS

In the course of this study one rather interesting question has arisen concerning the interrelationships of authors. Do individuals writing on the same subject have personal contact with others who share the same interests? An endeavor was made to discover whether there were personal contacts among the authors who emerged in this study. Special effort was made to document the personal contacts that did indeed exist among these authors, or if personal contact could not be determined, then it is shown that circumstances and situations existed which would have permitted personal contact, such as the fact that the dates when two individuals were at the same institution coincided, or they attended the same conference, or were members on the same committee.

The authors used are those 116 *personal* authors of works which were cited eight or more times who are listed in Part A of Appendix III, plus the nine authors listed in Part B of Appendix III, who were often cited but had no single work cited as many as eight times. This is a total of 125 personal authors whose professional careers range from the beginning of the nineteenth century to the present. This group consists of 85 Americans, 23 British, 9 Germans, 5 French, 1 Italian, 1 Indian, and 1 Yugoslav.

A hypothesis was made that there exist circumstances which would allow for the possibility and probability of a chain of personal contacts connecting this group of authors, and that each had the opportunity to have at least one personal contact with another individual in this set. As it turned out, many of these had contacts with quite a few of the others and no attempt has been made to document all possibilities, only that there existed the circumstances for a chain of contacts which would permit one to trace the interrelationships from Panizzi to those living today.

THE BEGINNING OF THE NETWORK OF RELATIONSHIPS

The first link in the chain that was uncovered begins with Sir Anthony Panizzi of the British Museum; he knew personally Edward Edwards, who also was at the British Museum, and Charles Jewett, who at the time of their meeting was the librarian at Brown University in Providence, Rhode Island. Panizzi's biographer, Louis Fagan, writes:

Panizzi, Thomas Watts, J. Winter Jones, Edward Edwards, and John H. Parry, formed a committee for framing the rules for the new General Catalogue of the whole Library; each of them was separately to prepare, according to his own views, rules for the compilation of the projected work. These were afterwards discussed collectively, and when any difference arose, it was settled by vote.[1]

In describing the events of 1853, Fagan noted that:

Professor Jewett had made Panizzi's acquaintance on his visit to London several years before, with the object of studying our Library....[2]

Jewett's biographer, Joseph Borome, confirms this connection with Panizzi:

Jewett then departed for England [1845] where for six months he repeated his course upon the Continent: he visited libraries and librarians, never failing to study their methods of constructing catalogs; ... For a period he was almost a daily frequenter of the British Museum, during which time he examined the management of its library thoroughly and formed an abiding friendship with the keeper of printed books (and later principal librarian), Anthony Panizzi.[3]

Jewett, in turn, knew Charles Ammi Cutter, despite the fact that Cutter was 21 years his junior. Both were at the Boston Public Library from 1860 until Jewett's death in 1868.[4] Borome writes that "... as the second decade of his superintendency opened, Jewett had on his agenda many projects, including a catalog of the Prince Library."[5] It was in this connection, during the period 1860 to 1868, that Jewett and Cutter were colleagues. At that time

"... young Cutter, not content with the absorbing duties of a cataloger in the [Harvard] college library, was also employed as a special assistant in the Boston Public Library. His particular task was to prepare for publication a catalog of the printed books in the library of the Reverend Thomas Prince, which was deposited in that institution.[6]

Thus the chain of contacts began. From this point there are many interrelations among the majority of our 125 authors of the set already defined.

INTERNATIONAL RELATIONSHIPS

Cutter and Melvil Dewey probably had their first encounter in 1873, at which time Cutter was Librarian of the Boston Atheneum and Dewey was Librarian at Amherst College. Dawe states that in February 1873 Dewey:

... reports his first talk with C. A. Cutter and remarks as an interesting point that: "He [Cutter] puts books on the horse under horse and not under zoology."[7]

Dewey and Cutter went to England to attend the International Library Conference held in London in October of 1877. According to the "List of members of the conference," also present were Henry Benjamin Wheatley of the Royal Society Library in London, and Leopold Delisle of the Bibliothèque Nationale in Paris.[8]

In 1897, they again crossed the Atlantic to attend the second International Library Conference held in London in July. The "List of members of the conference" includes another American, William Coolidge Lane representing the Boston Atheneum; a German professor from the Universitäts-Bibliothek at Göttingen, Karl Dziatzko; Leopold Delisle, administrator of the Bibliothèque Nationale in Paris; and three English librarians; Louis Stanley Jast (originally Jastrzebski[9]) of the Public Library of Peterborough; James Duff Brown, Librarian of the Clerkenwell Public Library in London; and John Henry Quinn, Librarian of the Public Libraries of Chelsea (London).[10]

During his long and active career, John Henry Quinn knew many prominent librarians, one obvious friend was Henry Waldo Acomb, who was the co-author of Quinn's book on cataloging and indexing.[11] Acomb was the librarian of the National Liberal Club in London until 1934, at which time he accepted the position of Librarian at the University of Durham.[12]

James Duff Brown went to the United States in 1893 to attend the International Congress of Librarians in Chicago and met many American librarians. About this trip to America, William Munford, Brown's biographer, says that "he was able to meet many of the prominent American librarians of the period, including Melvil Dewey, and to inspect not only libraries but also Dewey's controversial pioneer library school at Albany."[13]

Brown and Louis Stanley Jast first met at the Conference of the Library Association of the United Kingdom in Belfast in September of 1894.[14] Later, a true and lasting friendship developed, enabling James D. Stewart to write that:

> ... when Jast came to Croydon, he and J.D.B. soon became fast friends, and collaborators in furthering new movements. I remember J.D.B. telling me, with a twinkle in his eye, of a joint paper he and Jast were giving at a professional meeting: "I provide the sense and Jast provides the voice."[15]

In 1892 "... Peterborough chose Jast as its Chief Librarian out of 55 applicants...."[16] Six years later "... in July, 1898 Jast submitted his resignation at Peterborough following his appointment as Chief Librarian of the Croydon Public Libraries."[17]

Jast soon became a well-known figure in library circles and Croydon gained the reputation as one of the most advanced and innovative public libraries in Britain. In June of 1904, Jast was given a "... temporary appointment as Honorary Secretary..." of the Library Association.[18] "His obvious abilities and tremendous application quickly made good impressions on friends and critics alike and he was nominated also ... as the official delegate to the American Library Association Congress at St. Louis in October."[19] Jast's library committee at Croydon was pleased with his nomination and increased his annual leave to six weeks in order to facilitate his long trip. "Jast sailed for America at the end of September, 1904 and, after a rough crossing, was able to visit public libraries in New York, Brooklyn, Philadelphia and Pittsburgh and to spend three days at the Library of Congress. . . ." before going on to St. Louis.[20] "It is indeed fair to express the view that Jast and the veteran Melvil Dewey were the lions of the Congress," after which Jast visited Dewey's library school in Albany.[21] "The stimulus provided by Jast's first visit to America was lasting," and within three years Croydon had a "lady typist," and regular weekly meetings of senior staff members ". . . to discuss administrative and routine matters and to consider suggestions. . . ."[22]

During the years that Jast was Chief Librarian at Croydon (1898-1915) he had several very promising young men working under his direction, among them were: James D. Stewart, Maurice H. B. Mash, Ernest A. Savage, Henry A. Sharp, and Berwick Sayers, all of whom are highly cited authors in this study.

James D. Stewart, in his contribution to the Sayers festschrift, says that in 1904 Sayers "succeeded E. A. Savage as deputy librarian to Louis Stanley Jast at the Croydon Public Libraries."[23] Sayers was at the Croydon Public Libraries for almost all of his professional life.

> His experience as deputy librarian to Jast at Croydon came to an end in March 1915 when he was appointed Chief Librarian at Wallasey, once more succeeding E. A. Savage; but this brief interlude ended when he was recalled to Croydon to become its Chief Librarian in December of the same year, when Jast went to Manchester. He thus served the Croydon Public Libraries for over forty years, from 1904 to 1915 as Deputy and from 1915 to December 1947 as Chief Librarian.[24]

Upon Sayer's retirement from the Croydon Public Libraries in 1947,[25] Henry A. Sharp was appointed Chief Librarian,[26] and he remained in this post until he retired in 1951.[27]

The times at which Henry Sharp and Berwick Sayers were at Croydon are almost identical; Sharp was there for 38 years, from 1913 to 1951.[28]

James Douglas Stewart, who was James Duff Brown's nephew ". . . began his career at the Croydon Public Libraries where Stanley Jast was then in charge, where Dr. E. A. Savage and Berwick Sayers both served in those days, Stewart being a contemporary of the latter for a time."[29] It was impossible to determine when Stewart started to work at Croydon, but he was there in 1903.[30] In 1906 Stewart left Croydon and went to work for his uncle, James Duff Brown, at the Islington Public Libraries.[31] He remained at Islington until ". . . 1927 when he became Borough Librarian of the then Borough of Bermondsey, where he remained until retirement in 1950."[32]

Before his appointment as Borough Librarian and Curator of Burton-upon-Trent in 1918, Maurice H. B. Mash was also at Croydon Public Libraries, and ". . . held the position of Chief Assistant, Central Library, Croydon, and had served under both Mr. L. S. Jast and Mr. W. C. Berwick Sayers."[33] It was not possible to ascertain Mash's year of birth, nor the year in which he began at Croydon, but he was there in 1908 because he appeared in a group photograph of the library staff.[34]

Ernest Albert Savage began his library career at the Croydon Public Libraries at the early age of thirteen; his " . . . appointment is minuted 30th February, 1890."[35] He worked up to the rank of deputy librarian under Stanley Jast, but left Croydon in 1904 to go to Bromley.[36] From there he went to Wallasey and Coventry before becoming the Chief of the Edinburgh Public Libraries in 1922, where he remained until his retirement in 1942.[37]

A recapitulation of the careers of these six men who were associated with the Croydon Public Libraries shows that Ernest A. Savage was there when it first opened in 1890 and stayed until 1904; Louis Stanley Jast was the Chief Librarian from 1898 to 1915; Berwick Sayers was deputy librarian to Jast from 1904 to 1915, and Chief Librarian from 1915 until 1947; James D. Stewart went there sometime between 1898 and 1903, but he left in 1906; Maurice Mash was there in 1908 (and perhaps even a few years earlier) and remained until 1918; and Henry A. Sharp started at Croydon in 1913 and retired in 1951, after having served as its Chief Librarian from 1947 to 1951.

With so many outstanding librarians in its employ during such a long and eventful history it is no wonder that James Duff Brown's biographer, William A. Munford, could remark that the Croydon Public Libraries' " . . . influence on public library trends in such varied matters, among others to open access, classification and cataloguing, local collections, and work with children (to name no more than a few of the obvious) must be remembered an essential background to L.A. [Library Association] history in the early twentieth century."[38]

While at Croydon, Sayers also taught courses in practical classification at University College in London and one of his students was the late S. R. Ranganathan, the ". . . creator of the Colon Classification, and the man who has been called the father of the library movement in India."[39] Ranganathan commented on Sayers' book, *Introduction to library classification*, saying that as a student he ". . . had the benefit of being taught on its basis by Sayers himself," and further remarking that ". . . it was a privilege . . . to be in his class. He was a born teacher."[40]

In 1923 Sayers went to Paris to attend an international library conference and appearing in the "Liste des adhérents au congrès" is the name of Eugene Ledos, of the Department des Imprimés, Bibliothèque Nationale in Paris, who is one of the highly cited French authors, as well as that of Berwick Sayers.[41]

AMERICAN RELATIONSHIPS, 1876-1910

Relationships among the American group of frequently cited authors are also extensive. Melvil Dewey was the catalyst for the conference held in Philadelphia in 1876 out of which grew the American Library Association.[42] One of the librarians who was very active in this new organization was Frederic B. Perkins, who served with Charles A. Cutter, Boston Atheneum, and Frederick Jackson, Newton [Mass.] Free Library, in 1877 as an original member of the Co-operation Committee of the American Library Association.[43] Perkins was with the Boston Public Library from 1876 to 1880, and was librarian of the San Francisco Public Library from 1880 to 1887.[44] In a brief interlude between associations with these two libraries he was "... connected with Mr. Dewey in the Readers' and Writers' Economy Co.,"[45] which manufactured and distributed time-saving devices for librarians, and was the forerunner of the Library Bureau.[46] He also was one of the cooperating editors of the early volumes of the *Library Journal* of which Dewey was the first editor.[47]

Another librarian "... actively interested in the work and aims of the American Library Association...." was Klas August Linderfelt, who was "... practically the creator of the Milwaukee Public Library...."[48] Linderfelt served as a "councillor" of the American Library Association from 1882 until 1891.[49] In 1890 he was chosen as one of its vice-presidents.[50]

He was unique in many ways; first of all, he is the only nineteenth century American librarian of this group of 125 who was never associated with a library in either New York or New England. "In 1880 he was appointed librarian of the newly established Milwaukee Public Library, which opened in May of that year....";[51] this was the only library with which he was ever associated.

Secondly, Linderfelt was a prolific writer and contributed many articles to the *Library Journal* from 1881 to 1891. His most outstanding work was *Eclectic card catalog rules*. He had met Cutter very early in his library career, and in fact, it was Charles A. Cutter who appeared as the publisher in the imprint of Linderfelt's book.[52] In reviewing this book in 1891, William C. Lane of Harvard College wrote:

> Mr. Linderfelt has compiled and Mr. Cutter has published a work which all librarians who are familiar with Jewett's and Perkins's and Cutter's and Dewey's handbooks on the same subject, will be glad to place by the side of those books, and which those who do not own the earlier volumes will be glad to have in their stead to take the place in some measure of them all.[53]

This was very high praise indeed!

He attended many conferences of the American Library Association and the proceedings contain many of his comments and contributions. He was quite outspoken and apparently enjoyed considerable fame and popularity. On Friday, October 16, 1891, at the annual A.L.A. conference in San Francisco, he was elected as the seventh president of the Association, and William Fletcher of Amherst College Library was chosen as the vice-president.[54] But on April 28, 1892, scandal reared its ugly head. Linderfelt was arrested in Milwaukee for the embezzlement of public funds, and in May he resigned as President of A.L.A.[55] The Association's action was speedy. On May 21, 1892, the Executive Committee, consisting of Melvil Dewey, New York State Library School; Charles A. Cutter, Boston Atheneum; Frederick Crunden, St. Louis Public Library; Frank P. Hill, Free Public Library, Newark, New Jersey; and Hannah P. James, Ousterhout Free Public Library, Wilkes-Barre, Pennsylvania, met and erased the name of Klas August Linderfelt from the roster of A.L.A. presidents. This was done even though he had already held this office for more than six months.[56]

Such a scandal has been highly unusual among librarians who are generally considered to be quite sedate, prim and proper. Melvil Dewey, a dynamic and influential person, had reacted swiftly and helped maintain the respectability of the American Library Association. It was this same dynamic quality in Dewey's personality that attracted so many other outstanding persons to the profession and interested them in its growth and development.

As the founder of the world's first library school and originator of its best known library classification scheme (as well as contributor to many other aspects of the library profession), it is no wonder that Melvil Dewey had personal contacts with many prominent people, and no doubt he was a great "inspirer" as Dawe subtitles his biography.[57] In our group of 125 authors, of whom 85 are Americans, there are 11 who are graduates of the New York State Library School. Of these 11, there are 8 who studied there while Dewey was Director from 1887 to 1905.[58]

Melvil Dewey was the librarian of Columbia College when he opened *his* School of Library Economy there in 1887.[59] Fremont Rider describes this event by saying:

> It is typical of the paradoxes that marked all of Melvil Dewey's life that the world's first library school—his conception and creation—began where it was not wanted, was conducted from its very first day in direct violation of the explicit orders of the trustees of the college, was initiated without funds, without faculty, without equipment—in fact, without anything but students and enthusiasm.[60]

Many outstanding librarians were volunteer lecturers during the first year of the School of Library Economy at Columbia College and Dewey listed them in his first annual report, dated June 20, 1887. Among many others are the familiar names of Charles A. Cutter, Boston Atheneum; William I. Fletcher, Amherst College Library; and William Coolidge Lane, Harvard College.[61]

The Library School only lasted for two years at Columbia. "On December 20, 1888, Dewey's resignation as Columbia's librarian had been presented to the trustees of the college and, on January 7, 1889, it had been accepted."[62] "From January, 1889, when he moved to Albany, to 1899, Dewey was both Secretary of the Board of Regents and State Librarian. The School moved to Albany in April, 1889, and eventually became well known as the New York State Library School."[63]

Dewey had been forced to resign from Columbia College because he had been guilty of gross insubordination due to "his retention of women students in his library-school classes...," and this "... was in direct violation of the trustees' express prohibition."[64]

As mentioned above, a subsequently distinguished group of eight individuals attended the New York State Library School. The following is a list of their names, the years of attendance at the Library School, and their most outstanding professional positions. In order of their attendance they are: Aksel Josephson, 1893-1894, chief cataloger at the John Crerar Library from 1896 to 1923; Mary Wilson MacNair and Harriet Wheeler Pierson, 1895-1896—these two first cousins had identical professional careers, both were catalogers at the New York Public Library from 1896 to 1900, and then both were serial catalogers at the Library of Congress from 1900 until their retirement in 1942; Dorcas Fellows, 1895-1898, general assistant at the New York State Library from 1899 to 1925; Isadore G. Mudge, 1898-1900, reference librarian at Columbia University from 1910 to 1938; Nathaniel Goodrich, 1902-1904, librarian at Dartmouth College Library from 1912 to 1950; Sophie K. Hiss, 1904-1906, cataloger at the Cleveland Public Library from 1908 until 1943; and Fremont Rider, 1905-1906, librarian at Wesleyan University Library from 1933 to 1953.[65]

While a student, Fremont Rider claims to have served as a private secretary to Dewey.[66] In the preface to his biography of Dewey, Rider says:

> He remains the greatest man with whom I ever came into long-continued personal contact. Except for him I would never have entered the library profession. Except for him there would be no library profession (in the form we now know it) for me to enter![67]

Dorcas Fellows held several brief cataloging positions before going to the New York State Library in 1899, where she remained until 1925. She was also on the faculty of the New York State Library School and served as instructor during the years, 1911-1918 and 1922-1926.[68] During that period the other three students (who are among the most frequently cited authors) graduated from the Library School. Their names, the years of attendance at the Library School, and their most outstanding professional positions are: Ruth Wallace, 1913-1915, chief of the cataloging department of the Indianapolis Public Library from 1919 to 1947; Winifred Ver Nooy, 1913-1915, reference librarian at the University of Chicago Library from 1922 to 1956; and Caroline Whittemore, 1922-1923, cataloger at Dartmouth College Library from 1929 to 1956.[69]

Dorcas Fellows was the editor of the *Decimal classification* from 1921 until her death in 1938.[70] During this period she was quite active as a consultant on the Decimal Classification. For example, Margaret F. Johnson, another highly cited author, gave special thanks to Fellows in the introduction to her cataloging manual, saying: "... to Miss Dorkas Fellows, editor, Decimal Classification and Relative Index, special acknowledgement is made for ... valuable criticisms and suggestions as to changes and additions."[71]

An excellent example of the interrelationships of the authors under study is found in the preface to *The care and treatment of music in a library*, edited by Ruth Wallace. The sub-committee of the A.L.A. Committee on Cataloging, which was responsible for this publication, wrote:

> Of those who read the preliminary draft special acknowledgment is due ... Sophie K. Hiss, Cleveland Public Library; J. C. M. Hanson, University of Chicago, ... Dorcas Fellows, editor of the Decimal classification, gave expert advice concerning the subject of classification.[72]

Margaret Mann, Chairman of the A.L.A. Committee on Cataloging, 1926-1927, also wrote a part of the preface saying:

> To T. Franklin Currier, Chairman of the Committee on Cataloging, 1924-26, acknowledgment is due for revising the manuscript.[73]

The graduates of the New York State Library School went to widely scattered libraries and had professional contacts with persons from many parts of the United States. Sophie K. Hiss, who received her library degree in 1906, had three brief positions before she went to the Cleveland Public Library as a cataloger in 1908. She worked there until her retirement in 1943.[74] Another of the highly cited authors, Florence M. Gifford, joined Miss Hiss at the Cleveland Public Library in 1909, where she remained until her retirement in 1957.[75] She received a diploma from the library school at Western Reserve University in 1911.

As we have seen, Aksel Josephson graduated from the New York State Library School in 1894 and accepted a position as cataloger in the Lenox Library and the New York Public Library.[76] When he left New York in 1896 to accept the position of head cataloger at the John Crerar Library in Chicago he had worked up to the position of head cataloger at the Lenox Library.[77] At the time that Josephson began his career in New York, Miss Theresa Hitchler was the chief cataloger of the New York Free Circulating Library,[78] and with such similar interests and positions it seems highly likely that they met at some time before Josephson went to Chicago.

As far as can be determined Theresa Hitchler began her library career in the late 1880's. She was in charge of the Bruce Free Library, a branch of the New York Free Circulating Library, when it opened in 1888.[79] By 1892 she was working as a cataloger in the New York Free Circulating Library, and was no longer in charge of a branch library.[80] Her library career ended when she resigned (retired?) from the Brooklyn Public Library in 1928.[81] Evidently she was very dedicated to her career as a cataloger. Lydenberg, in his history of the New York Public Library, describes the establishment of the St. Agnes Free Library in 1894 in New York City:

> In the spring of that year the librarian, assisted by Miss Theresa Hitchler, then chief cataloguer for the New York Free Circulating Library, working at night in addition to her regular work, and serving without pay, recatalogued and reclassified the collection.[82]

During her last four years as chief cataloger of the New York Free Circulating Library the head librarian was another of the often cited authors, Dr. Arthur E. Bostwick. He held this position from April 1, 1895 to March 8, 1899.[83] In 1897 Bostwick was elected President of the New York Library Club and Theresa Hitchler was chosen Treasurer.[84] On March 8, 1899 Bostwick ". . . was chosen librarian of the newly formed Brooklyn Public Library. . . ."[85] It was also at this time that Hitchler resigned from the New York Free Circulating Library to accept the position of head cataloger at the new Brooklyn Public Library.[86]

Hitchler remained at Brooklyn until she left the profession in 1928, but Bostwick only stayed there for two years. In 1901 the New York Free Circulating Library became the Circulation Department of the New York Public Library,[87] and "... on March 1, 1901, Dr. Bostwick returned from Brooklyn to become Chief of the Circulation Department."[88]

Arthur E. Bostwick was President of the American Library Association for the 1907-1908 term, during which period T. Franklin Currier, Harvard University Library; William I. Fletcher, Amherst College Library; James C. M. Hanson, Library of Congress; and William Coolidge Lane, Harvard University Library, were all active in affairs of the Association and serving on various committees.[89] So the multiplicity of interconnections grows.

SUMMARY

Thus far, many contacts among our authors during the nineteenth century and early part of the twentieth have been documented, and in many other cases where documentation was not possible, situations and circumstances have been pointed out in which there existed both the possibility and probability for personal contact.

The importance of the role of discussion and interpersonal relationships in the development of professional ideas and opinions could not be better expressed than in the words of Stewart in his memorial essay on Sayers:

> I knew Sayers in a great variety of circumstances. From that first day in 1904 when he arrived from Bournemouth, to take up the position of deputy librarian at Croydon, we were friends. We talked endlessly about libraries as they were and as they might be; we worked and played and travelled together; and we fought the battle of the new librarianship at every meeting of our colleagues.[90]

FOOTNOTES

1. Fagan, Louis. *The life of Sir Anthony Panizzi, K.C.B., late Principal Librarian of the British Museum, Senator of Italy, &c, &c*. London, Remington, 1880. Vol. I, p. 168.
2. *Ibid.*, p. 170.
3. Borome, Joseph A. *Charles Coffin Jewett*. Chicago, American Library Association, 1951. p. 14.
4. Jewett's second decade began in 1868, and Borome writes: "On New Year's Day, 1868, Jewett looked back upon ten years of administering the affairs of the Boston Public Library." *Ibid.*, p. 161.
5. *Ibid.*, p. 166.
6. Cutter, William Parker. *Charles Ammi Cutter*. Chicago, American Library Association, 1931. p. 14.
7. Dawe, Grosvenor. *Melvil Dewey: seer, inspirer, doer, 1851-1931*. Essex Co., N.Y., Lake Placid, 1932. p. 158.

8. International Library Conference, 1st, London, 1877. *Transactions and proceedings*. London, 1878. pp. 253-258.

9. Concerning this name change Jast's biographers write: "The third Jastrzebski son . . . born on 20th August, 1868 . . . was given the name Louis Stanley. He retained his full Polish surname until 1895 when, following the suggestion of James Duff Brown, that so apparently unpronounceable a combination of consonants might hinder his career and kindness to his associates would be shown by amending it, he decided to use the first syllable only, pronouncing it Jast and not Yast as in Polish." Fry, Walter George and William A. Munford. *Louis Stanley Jast; a biographical sketch*. London, The Library Association, 1966. p. 2.

10. International Library Conference, 2d, London, 1897. *Transactions and proceedings*. London, 1898. pp. 259-272.

11. Quinn, John Henry and Henry Waldo Acomb. *A manual of cataloguing and indexing*. London, Allen & Unwin, 1933. 286p. (2d ed., Allen & Unwin, 1937.)

12. "Personal news," *Library world*, 37:58, August-September 1934.

13. Munford, William Arthur. *James Duff Brown, 1862-1914; portrait of a library pioneer*. London, The Library Association, 1968. p. 27.

14. *Ibid.*, p. 36.

15. Stewart, James D. " 'J.D.B.' and the 'L.W.' " *Library world*, 63:56, September 1961.

16. Fry, Walter G. and William A. Munford. *Louis Stanley Jast*. p. 7.

17. *Ibid.*, p. 16.

18. *Ibid.*, p. 27.

19. *Ibid.*

20. *Ibid.*, p. 28

21. *Ibid.*, p. 29.

22. *Ibid.*

23. Stewart, James D. "Sayers." In: Foskett, D. J. and B. I. Palmer, eds. *The Sayers memorial volume; essays in librarianship in memory of William Charles Berwick Sayers*. London, The Library Association, 1961. p. 14.

24. *Ibid.*, p. 15.

25. McColvin, Lionel R. " 'W.C.B.S.' ," *Librarian and book world*, 36:273, December 1947.

26. "Appointments and retirements," *Library Association record*, 49:239, September 1947.

27. "The retirement of Mr. Henry A. Sharp," *Library world*, 53:210, March 1951.

28. *Ibid.*

29. Thorne, W. Benson. "Stewart," *Library Association record*, 67:210, June 1965.

30. Stewart, James D. "The Library in fiction," *Library world*, 6:126-130, November 1903.

31. Munford, William A. *James Duff Brown*. p. 70.

32. Thorne, W. Benson. "Stewart," p. 211.

33. "De mortuis," *Librarian and book world*, 32:62, December 1942.
34. "Notable libraries: Croydon," *Library world*, 11:222-228, December 1908.
35. Savage, Ernest A. *A librarians' memories, portraits & reflections*. London, Grafton, 1952. pp. 56 and 80.
36. Munford, William A. *James Duff Brown*. p. 66.
37. Minto, Charles S. "Ernest A. Savage, LL.D., F.L.A.," *Library Association record*, 68:111, March 1966.
38. Munford, William A. "The Library Association in the twentieth century: selected aspects." In: Foskett, D. J. and B. I. Palmer, eds. *The Sayers memorial volume*. p. 28.
39. "People," *Library journal*, 97:3673, November 15, 1972.
40. Ranganathan, S. R. "Library classification on the march." In: Foskett, D. J. and B. I. Palmer. *The Sayers memorial volume*. p. 77.
41. Congrès International des Bibliothécaires et des Bibliophiles, Paris, 1923. *Procès-verbaux et mémoires*. Paris, Jouve, 1925. pp. 21-45.
42. Dawe, Grosvenor. *Melvil Dewey*. p. 174.
43. "American Library Association Executive Board," *Library journal*, 2:221, November-December 1877.
44. "Librarians," *Library journal*, 24:82, February, 1899.
45. *Ibid.*
46. Dawe, Grosvenor. *Melvil Dewey*. p. 183.
47. *Ibid.*, p. 257.
48. "Librarians," *Library journal*, 25:194, April 1900.
49. "Officers and Executive Board of the American Library Association, 1882-83," *Library journal*, 8:305, September-October 1883; "Organization of the American Library Association, 1883-84," *Library journal*, 9:5, January 1884; "Officers of the American Library Association," *Library journal*, 10:347, September-October 1885; "Officers for the ensuing year," *Library journal*, 11:371, August-September 1886; "Officers of the American Library Association for 1887-88," *Library journal*, 12:449, September-October 1887; "Officers of the American Library Association for 1889-90," *Library journal*, 14:283, May-June 1889; "Officers for the ensuing year," *Library journal*, 15:C137, December 1890.
50. "Officers for the ensuing year," *Library journal*, 15:C137, December 1890.
51. "Librarians," *Library journal*, 25:194, April 1900.
52. Linderfelt, Klas August. *Eclectic card catalog rules; author and title entries*. Boston, Charles A. Cutter, 1890. 104p. The verso of the title page reads: "Copyright, 1890, by C. A. Cutter."
53. "Reviews," *Library journal*, 16:148-149, May 1891.
54. "Resolutions," *Library journal*, 16:C123, December 1891.
55. "Librarians," *Library journal*, 25:194, April 1900.
56. "Meeting of Executive Committee," *Library journal*, 17:386, September 1892. "On motion the action of the Secretary was approved, the resignation of K. A. Linderfelt was accepted, to take effect from the time of election, and the Secretary was directed to record W. I. Fletcher as President for the entire term."

57. Dawe, Grosvenor. *Melvil Dewey: seer, inspirer, doer; 1851-1931*. Essex Co., N.Y., Lake Placid Club, 1932. 391p.
58. New York State Library School. *Register, 1887-1926*. James I. Wyer memorial edition. New York, New York State Library School Association, 1959. p. lvii.
59. Dawe, Grosvenor. *Melvil Dewey*. p. 191.
60. Rider, Fremont. *Melvil Dewey*. Chicago, American Library Association, 1944. p. 41.
61. Dawe, Grosvenor. *Melvil Dewey*. pp. 194-195.
62. Rider, Fremont. *Melvil Dewey*. p. 50.
63. *Ibid.*, p. 53.
64. *Ibid.*, p. 50.
65. New York State Library School. *Register, 1887-1926*. pp. 21, 27, 36, 53, 63, 69, and 180.
66. *Who's who in library service; a biographical directory of professional librarians of the United States and Canada*. 3d ed. New York, Grolier, 1955. p. 409.
67. Rider, Fremont. *Melvil Dewey*. p. viii.
68. New York State Library School. *Register, 1887-1926*. p. 26. Note: Her full name was Jennie Dorcas Fellows, but she used Dorkas Fellows, thus following the simplification advocated by the Spelling Reform Association of which Melvil Dewey was Secretary. For this reason one finds her name written both as Dorcas and Dorkas.
69. *Ibid.*, pp. 106 and 146.
70. *Ibid.*, p. 26.
71. Johnson, Margaret Fullerton. *Manual of cataloging and classification for elementary school libraries*. New York, Wilson, 1929. p. vi.
72. Wallace, Ruth, editor. *The care and treatment of music in a library*. Chicago, American Library Association, 1927. p. 6.
73. *Ibid.*, p. 7.
74. New York State Library School. *Register, 1887-1926*. p. 63.
75. "Retirements," *Library journal*, 82:2513, October 15, 1957.
76. New York State Library School. *Register, 1887-1926*. p. 21.
77. "Librarians," *Library journal*, 21:119, March 1896.
78. Lydenberg, Harry M. *History of the New York Public Library: Astor, Lenox and Tilden Foundations*. New York, New York Public Library, 1923. p. 271.
79. "The Bruce Library," *Library journal*, 13:18, January 1888.
80. "Attendance register," *Library journal*, 17:C101, August 1892.
81. "Among librarians," *Library journal*, 53:916, November 1, 1928.
82. Lydenberg, Harry M. *History of the New York Public Library*. p. 271.
83. *Ibid.*, p. 234.
84. "New York Library Club," *Library journal*, 22:266, May 1897.
85. Lydenberg, Harry M. *History of the New York Public Library*. p. 234.
86. *Ibid.*, p. 226.

87. *Ibid.*, p. 405.
88. *Ibid.*, p. 234.
89. American Library Association handbook. "Committees, 1907-08." In: *A.L.A. bulletin*, 1:H13-14, September 1907.
90. Stewart, James D. "Sayers." In: Foskett, D. J. and B. I. Palmer, eds. *The Sayers memorial volume*. p. 15.

CHAPTER VI

INTERRELATIONSHIPS AMONG THE MOST CITED AUTHORS: INSTITUTIONS (DATA)

In the preceding chapter personal relationships were documented among many catalogers who appear in the list of frequently cited authors. In a few cases where documentation was not possible, circumstances were pointed out where personal contact was highly probable. On the list of the most cited authors there are many who are of the twentieth century, and it is easier to point out contacts, or probabilities thereof, through the simultaneous presence of individuals at the same institution rather than from individual to individual.

Several British institutions were mentioned in Chapter V with which some of the authors had been connected. The most important one being the Croydon Public Libraries. During the first decade of the twentieth century six of our 23 British authors were employed there. Sir Anthony Panizzi and Edward Edwards were at the British Museum, and the Islington Public Libraries employed James Duff Brown and James D. Stewart.

AMERICAN RELATIONSHIPS THROUGH INSTITUTIONS

After the turn of the century, the number and size of libraries increased greatly and at a rapid rate. The profession of librarianship was also developing at a quick pace. At this point it is possible to indicate the opportunities for personal contact between *groups* of individuals who were at the same institution simultaneously. There are ten institutions with which more than one-half of the 125 personal authors were at one time or another connected, perhaps as instructor, librarian or student. The lists which follow contain only individuals whose presence in one of these ten institutions coincided with at least one other person, in order to form the longest possible continuous chain of probable contacts.

In each list there is the name of at least one person whose name also appears in the succeeding list, thus giving a horizontal linkage between the lists. As might be expected, within each list there is a continuous overlapping of years between the periods in which individuals were associated in one capacity or another with that institution, thus giving a vertical continuity among the persons who were at a given institution.

The ten institutions are: Library of Congress, University of California at Berkeley, University of Chicago, University of North Carolina, University of Michigan, New York Public Library, Harvard University, Columbia University,

University of Illinois, and Yale University. Of the 85 Americans who are among the most cited authors, 69 (81%) have been associated at one time or another with one or more of these institutions. This is quite an impressive number.

There are 62 librarians who make up the *continuous chains* of these institutions. (Outside of these ten, no attempt has been made to show the other institutions with which the same 62 persons may have been associated.) It should be noted that seven famous names are absent from the lists: Dewey, who was at one time librarian at Columbia University; Perkins, who at one time studied at Yale; Cutter and Lane, who were at Harvard; Josephson, Bostwick, MacNair, and Pierson who were at the New York Public Library; and Wallace, who spent a summer at the University of Chicago. They have not been included here because they were treated in the previous chapter, and because the years they were present at those institutions would not form a continuous link with the other 62 individuals discussed in this chapter.

There is no indication made as to whether the person was affiliated with the library or the library school of the universities listed herein. Quite often persons were associated with both. Also, many of these librarians have been in the role of student, practitioner and instructor in the same institution, and several have had two roles simultaneously. In order to reduce complexity, no indication is given as to the role of the individual at that institution. There may also appear to be conflicts in the years of service of some of the 62 authors. This is due to the fact that many worked in one institution and taught at another, or were associated simultaneously with another in a different capacity.

Even though every effort has been made to list the complete years during which an individual was at a given institution, it was not always possible to determine duration because of the paucity of biographical data for many persons. However, any years indicated were verified. These are as accurate as possible and they do provide the necessary linkage, which was the primary objective in making the lists. It is possible that some have been at an institution longer than indicated, but none were there less.[1]

LIST 1
LIBRARY OF CONGRESS

Hanson, James C. M.	1897-1910
Martel, Charles	1897-1945
Phillips, Philip Lee	1897-1920
MacNair, Mary Wilson	1900-1942
Pierson, Harriet W.	1900-1942
Bishop, William W.	1907-1915
Childs, James B.	1925-1955
Fellows, Dorcas	1927-1937
Morsch, Lucile M.	1940-1966
Ellinger, Werner B.	1941-1969

LIST 1 (cont'd)

Henkle, Herman H.	1942-1947
Lubetzky, Seymour	1943-1960
Custer, Benjamin	1944-1946
	and
	1956-1969
Gull, Cloyd Dake	1945-1952
Angell, Richard S.	1946-1969
Reichmann, Felix	1946-1947
Spalding, C. Sumner	1946-1969

LIST 2
UNIVERSITY OF CALIFORNIA AT BERKELEY

Nyholm, Amy Wood	1930-1941
Hand, Elinor	1930
Henkle, Herman H.	1930-1935
Taube, Mortimer	1932-1935

LIST 3
UNIVERSITY OF CHICAGO

Hanson, James C. M.	1910-1934
Ver Nooy, Winifred	1912-1956
Howe, Harriet Emma	1927-1931
Randall, William M.	1929-1947
Van Hoesen, Henry B.	1929-1931
	and
	1939-1949
Taube, Mortimer	1931
Akers, Susan G.	1932
Wilson, Louis R.	1932-1942
Coney, Donald	1933-1934
Haygood, William C.	1934-1939
	and
	1947-1948
Ellsworth, Ralph	1934-1937
Miller, Robert A.	1934-1936
Mishoff, Willard O.	1936-1937
Tauber, Maurice	1939-1944
Swank, Raynard Coe	1941-1944
Reichmann, Felix	1942

LIST 3 (cont'd)

Berthold, Arthur B.	1945-1948
Henkle, Herman H.	1950-1969
Strout, Ruth French	1954-1969

LIST 4
UNIVERSITY OF NORTH CAROLINA

Wilson, Louis R.	1901-1932
	and
	1942-1945
Coney, Donald	1928-1932
Akers, Susan G.	1931-1954
Burch, Vella Jane	1935-1936

LIST 5
UNIVERSITY OF MICHIGAN

Bishop, William W.	1915-1941
Coney, Donald	1920-1927
Randall, William M.	1923-1925
Gjelsness, Rudolph H.	1925-1928
	and
	1937-1964
Mann, Margaret	1926-1943
Mishoff, Willard O.	1930-1931
Colvin, Laura C.	1934
Gull, Cloyd Dake	1936-1939
Haskins, Susan	1937
Osborn, Andrew D.	1937-1938
Branscomb, Harvie	1939

LIST 6
NEW YORK PUBLIC LIBRARY

Metcalf, Keyes D.	1913-1937
Akers, Susan G.	1917 and
	1920
MacPherson, Harriet D.	1917 and
	1930-1931
Dean, Hazel	1924-1928

LIST 6 (cont'd)

Wright, Wyllis E.	1927-1930 and 1933-1945
Osborn, Andrew D.	1928-1938
Gjelsness, Rudolph H.	1928-1932
Morsch, Lucile M.	1929
Miller, Robert A.	1930-1931
Custer, Benjamin	1932-1939
Berthold, Arthur B.	1935-1936
Ellinger, Werner B.	1937-1939
Kingery, Robert E.	1937-1965

LIST 7
HARVARD UNIVERSITY

Currier, T. Franklin	1894-1933
Haskins, Susan	1929-1969
Dean, Hazel	1930-1939
Spalding, C. Sumner	1933
Metcalf, Keyes D.	1937-1955
Osborn, Andrew D.	1938-1958
Thom, Ian Walter	1947-1951

LIST 8
COLUMBIA UNIVERSITY

Mudge, Isadore G.	1911-1934
MacPherson, Harriet D.	1917-1924 and 1927-1943
Alvord, Dorothy	1919-1920
Howe, Harriet Emma	1920-1923
Mishoff, Willard O.	1927-1928
Metcalf, Keyes D.	1928-1933
Allez, George C.	1929-1932
Miller, Robert A.	1929-1930
MacDonald, M. Ruth	1929-1930
Gjelsness, Rudolph H.	1930-1932
Hanson, James C. M.	1930-1934
Van Hoesen, Henry B.	1933 and 1946-1947

LIST 8 (cont'd)

Angell, Richard S.	1934-1946
Osborn, Andrew D.	1934 and
	1940-1943
Tauber, Maurice	1934-1938
	and
	1944-1969
Jackson, Sidney L.	1936-1941
	and
	1949-1950
Morsch, Lucile M.	1937-1939
Wright, Wyllis E.	1939-1945
Ellinger, Werner B.	1939-1940
Whittemore, Caroline	1940-1941
Thom, Ian Walter	1940-1946
Colvin, Laura C.	1945-1946
Herrick, Mary D.	1947-1948

LIST 9
UNIVERSITY OF ILLINOIS

Trotier, Arnold H.	1925-1969
Lewis, Dorothy C.	1928
Dunkin, Paul S.	1935-1937
Henkle, Herman H.	1935-1937
Colvin, Laura C.	1939
Watkins, David Roy	1940-1941
Strout, Ruth French	1942-1943

LIST 10
YALE UNIVERSITY

Field, F. Bernice	1931-1939
	and
	1944-1966
Pettee, Julia	1939-1946
Watkins, David Roy	1956-1965

Table 12 lists alphabetically the 62 persons that appear in the preceding lists. At the right of each name are indicated those institutions with which that individual was associated.

The key to the symbols used is:

CAL = University of California at Berkeley
CHI = University of Chicago
COL = Columbia University
HAR = Harvard University
IL = University of Illinois
LC = Library of Congress
MI = University of Michigan
NC = University of North Carolina
NY = New York Public Library
YA = Yale University

TABLE 12

Authors and the Institutions With
Which They Were Associated

Part A—Alphabetical arrangement of the
authors given in Lists 1-10

1.	Akers, Susan G.	CHI, NC, NY
2.	Allez, George C.	COL
3.	Alvord, Dorothy M.	COL
4.	Angell, Richard	COL, LC
5.	Berthold, Arthur	CHI, NY
6.	Bishop, William W.	LC, MI
7.	Branscomb, Harvie	MI
8.	Burch, Vella Jane	NC
9.	Childs, James B.	LC
10.	Colvin, Laura C.	COL, IL, MI
11.	Coney, Donald	CHI, MI, NC
12.	Currier, T. Franklin	HA
13.	Custer, Benjamin	LC, NY
14.	Dean, Hazel	HA, NY
15.	Dunkin, Paul S.	IL
16.	Ellinger, Werner B.	COL, LC, NY
17.	Ellsworth, Ralph E.	CHI
18.	Fellows, Dorcas	LC
19.	Field, F. Bernice	YA
20.	Gjelsness, Rudolph H.	COL, MI, NY
21.	Gull, Cloyd Dake	LC, MI
22.	Hand, Elinor	CAL

50

TABLE 12 (cont'd)

23.	Hanson, James C. M.	CHI, COL, LC
24.	Haskins, Susan	HA, MI
25.	Haygood, William C.	CHI
26.	Henkle, Herman H.	CAL, CHI, IL, LC
27.	Herrick, Mary D.	COL
28.	Howe, Harriet E.	CHI, COL
29.	Jackson, Sidney L.	COL
30.	Kingery, Robert E.	NY
31.	Lewis, Dorothy	IL
32.	Lubetzky, Seymour	LC
33.	MacDonald, M. Ruth	COL
34.	MacNair, Mary Wilson	LC
35.	MacPherson, Harriet D.	COL, NY
36.	Mann, Margaret	MI
37.	Martel, Charles	LC
38.	Metcalf, Keyes D.	COL, HA, NY
39.	Miller, Robert A.	CHI, COL, NY
40.	Mishoff, Willard O.	CHI, COL, MI
41.	Morsch, Lucile M.	COL, LC, NY
42.	Mudge, Isadore G.	COL
43.	Nyholm, Amy	CAL
44.	Osborn, Andrew D.	COL, HA, MI, NY
45.	Pettee, Julia	YA
46.	Phillips, Philip L.	LC
47.	Pierson, Harriet	LC
48.	Randall, William M.	CHI, MI
49.	Reichmann, Felix	CHI, LC
50.	Spalding, C. Sumner	HA, LC
51.	Strout, Ruth F.	CHI, IL
52.	Swank, Raynard	CHI
53.	Taube, Mortimer	CAL, CHI
54.	Tauber, Maurice	CHI, COL
55.	Thom, Ian	COL, HA
56.	Trotier, Arnold H.	IL
57.	Van Hoesen, Henry B.	CHI, COL
58.	Ver Nooy, Winifred	CHI
59.	Watkins, David Roy	IL, YA
60.	Whittemore, Caroline	COL
61.	Wilson, Louis R.	CHI, NC
62.	Wright, Wyllis E.	COL, NY

TABLE 12 (cont'd)

Part B—Individuals associated with the ten institutions at times not overlapping with those for the above group

63.	Bostwick, Arthur Elmore	NY
64.	Cutter, Charles Ammi	HA
65.	Dewey, Melvil	COL
66.	Josephson, Aksel	NY
67.	Lane, William C.	HA
68.	Perkins, Frederic B.	YA
69.	Wallace, Ruth	CHI

SUMMARY

Quantitative data have been developed here regarding the institutional affiliation of the 85 Americans among the 125 personal authors of this study. There are 69 Americans who are shown to have been affiliated with only 10 institutions. Furthermore, 62 of the 69 form a continuous chain of overlapping presence at these institutions. Analysis and comment upon this interesting discovery are discussed in the next chapter.

FOOTNOTES

1. The basic tools used to document the data in the following lists were biographical directories of librarians:

Who's who in library service. Edited by C. C. Williamson and Alice L. Jewett. New York, Wilson, 1933. 457p.

Who's who in library service. Edited by C. C. Williamson and Alice L. Jewett. 2d ed. New York, Wilson, 1943. 612p.

Who's who in library service; a biographical directory of professional librarians of the United States and Canada. 3rd ed. Dorothy Ethlyn Cole, editor. New York, Grolier, 1955. 546p.

Who's who in library service; a biographical directory of professional librarians in the United States and Canada. Lee Ash, editor, 4th ed. Hamden, Conn., Shoe String Press, 1966. 776p.

A biographical directory of librarians in the United States and Canada. Lee Ash, editor. Chicago, A.L.A., 1970. 1250p.

Landau, Thomas, ed. *Who's who in librarianship.* Cambridge, Bowes & Bowes, 1954. 269p.

CHAPTER VII

INTERRELATIONSHIPS AMONG THE MOST CITED AUTHORS: INSTITUTIONS (ANALYSIS)

In the entire group of 125 personal authors, there are 85 who are Americans. In the previous chapter the personal history of each was examined and so far it has been possible to show that 69 (81%) of the 85 were connected at one time or another with only ten institutions. In rank order by the number of the 69 authors which were at each institution they are:[1]

Columbia University	24
University of Chicago	20
Library of Congress	17
New York Public Library	17
University of Michigan	11
Harvard University	9
University of Illinois	7
University of North Carolina	4
University of California at Berkeley	4
Yale University	4

The lists given in the preceding chapter do not supply conclusive proof that each of the 62 individuals knew at least one of the others, but they do provide proof of opportunity and indicate the strong probability that there were personal contacts.

The 85 Americans in this study represent 68% of the 125 personal authors. They can be categorized into two basic groups: the "outsiders" and the "insiders." The "outsiders" consist of those 16 Americans who were never associated with any of the ten institutions mentioned in Chapter VI. Nine of these individuals were treated in Chapter V, viz., William Fletcher, Florence Gifford, Nathaniel Goodrich, Sophie Hiss, Theresa Hitchler (who was Chief cataloger at the New York Free Circulating Library *before* it merged with the New York Public Library), Charles Jewett, Margaret F. Johnson, Klas Linderfelt and Fremont Rider. The remaining seven "outsiders" (Winona Adams, Emma Baldwin, Samuel Boggs, Bertha Buelow, Ralph Hagedorn, William Marcus and Watson O'Dell Pierce) will be discussed in Chapter VIII.

The other group, the "insiders," consist of those 69 persons who were *at one time or another* connected with one or more of the ten institutions listed in the preceding chapter. Upon further examination of the institutions with which these 69 persons were associated, it becomes evident that 56 (81%) of these librarians were associated with just five institutions, viz., the Library of Congress, New York Public Library, Columbia University and the Universities of Chicago and Michigan. These 56 Americans may be called the "inside insiders." This means that of the total 125 personal authors in this study that 56 (45%) were at one time or another associated with one or more of these five institutions!

This group of "insiders" should not be construed as an "invisible college." The individuals who were associated with the ten institutions may all be considered as "insiders," but only because of this association. All were members of "invisible colleges," but not all belonged to the same "invisible college." The various groups of "invisible colleges" form a chain from 1876 down to the present day. These "insiders" and some of the "outsiders" were members of various "invisible colleges." According to Diana Crane an "invisible college" is ". . . a social circle consisting of numerous direct and indirect ties. . . ."[2] The interrelationships of our frequently cited authors have shown many direct and indirect ties. The most outstanding individuals, who were undoubtedly focal points of various "invisible colleges," are: Melvil Dewey, William W. Bishop, James C. M. Hanson, Louis R. Wilson, Andrew D. Osborn and Seymour Lubetzky. Fremont Rider is a good example of an "outsider" who definitely was a member of the "invisible college" of which Melvil Dewey was the central figure. Rider knew Dewey personally, but was never associated with one of the ten institutions.

An analysis of the periods when the 56 persons were associated with each of these five institutions brings out some interesting patterns. For example, during the period 1928 to 1939, none of the 56 went to the Library of Congress, but were flocking to the other four institutions as librarians, instructors or students. Then in the 1940's many of these individuals went to the Library of Congress and several are still there.

A breakdown by individual institution is even more illuminating. The Graduate Library School of the University of Chicago was established in 1928, with James C. M. Hanson as its first professor.[3] Louis R. Wilson was the director of the Graduate Library School from 1932 to 1942. During this decade at least 15 of the 85 Americans were associated with the University of Chicago. However, only three others from this group have become associated with the University of Chicago since Wilson left there in 1942 to go to the University of North Carolina.

William W. Bishop left the Library of Congress in 1915 to become the director of the University of Michigan Library. He was placed in charge of the library school when it opened there in 1926. It was then that Margaret Mann joined its faculty to teach cataloging.[4] Mann had just returned to the United States from Paris where she had spent the previous two years teaching cataloging at "the Ecole des Bibliothècaires or Paris Library School, as it is generally called in English. . . ."[5] Margaret Mann retired in 1938,[6] and Bishop in 1941.[7] After their retirements only one person from our list of authors was at Michigan. This was Rudolph Gjelsness, who taught at the University of Michigan Library School from 1937 until he resigned in 1964. Other than Gjelsness, no other person from the group of 85 Americans has been at the University of Michigan since Mann and Bishop retired.

The period in which many of these individuals were at Columbia University was approximately from 1920 to 1945. It was in 1926 that the New York

State Library School at Albany and the library school of the New York Public Library were merged to form the new School of Library Service at Columbia University.[8] This seems to have attracted many of our frequently cited authors to Columbia. But since 1950 only one from this group, Maurice Tauber, has been connected with Columbia University.

Quite a few of these often cited authors were at the New York Public Library during the 1920's and 1930's. But by the end of 1939 there was only one person from our list who was still at the New York Public Library. This was Robert Kingery, who went there in 1937 and remained until 1965. After 1937 no other person from this group has been associated with the New York Public Library.

If, which seems justified by the evidence, one were to consider these 85 Americans as important contributors to the field of cataloging, and *if*, which also seems reasonable, their connection with an institution could be interpreted as a measure of importance of that institution's contribution to the field, *then* the following statements could be made.

The important institutions in cataloging during the first half of the twentieth century in rank order have been: Columbia University, University of Chicago, Library of Congress, New York Public Library, and the University of Michigan. At the beginning of the twentieth century only the Library of Congress had many prominent catalogers. Then during the late 1910's the New York Public Library assumed some prominence, but did not reach the level of the Library of Congress. However, during the late 1920's and the 1930's the University of Chicago and Columbia University surpassed the Library of Congress and became the principal American institutions in the field of cataloging. Also during the 1930's, the University of Michigan and the New York Public Library reached their heydays (so far as cataloging is concerned), but they were at a considerably lower level than Columbia and Chicago.

Only five of the 85 American authors were at the Library of Congress in the 1930's and no new person went there in that entire decade. However, since 1940 the Library of Congress has again taken the lead as the greatest contributor to the area of cataloging, far surpassing Chicago and Columbia. From 1950 to the present the Library of Congress has remained in the lead, and there has been almost no other competition from any other institution.

Many of these authors have held prominent positions, such as directors of libraries and library schools, but the honor of being recognized by one's own colleagues is also a measure of their influence. Thirteen of the most frequently cited authors have received the "Margaret Mann Citation in Cataloging and Classification"[9] since its inception in 1951. Their names and the year they were awarded the Citation are:[10]

Morsch, Lucile M.	1951
Tauber, Maurice F.	1953
Lubetzky, Seymour	1955
Akers, Susan G.	1956
Osborn, Andrew D.	1959
MacDonald, M. Ruth	1960

Wright, Wyllis E.	1962
Chaplin, Arthur H.	1963
Colvin, Laura C.	1965
Field, F. Bernice	1966
Spalding, C. Sumner	1967
Dunkin, Paul S.	1968
Ranganathan, S. R.	1970

Almost all of these people have served together on committees of the American Library Association and other organizations, or have been on joint panels, seminars, conferences and the like. All of the above, except Susan G. Akers, were very active in the conferences on catalog code revision preceding the publication of the Anglo-American cataloging code in 1967.[11]

As a concluding illustration of the great amount of personal contacts that some of these librarians must have had, it should be pointed out that ten of them have been elected President of the American Library Association and six have been elected President of the (British) Library Association. Their names and the years they presided as President are:

American Library Association[12]

Cutter, Charles A.	1887-1889
Dewey, Melvil	1890-July 1891, and June 1892-July 1893
Linderfelt, Klas A.	October 1891-May 1892
Fletcher, William I.	May 1892
Lane, William C.	1898-1899
Bostwick, Arthur E.	1907-1908
Bishop, William W.	1918-1919
Wilson, Louis R.	1935-1936
Metcalf, Keyes D.	1942-1943
Morsch, Lucile M.	1957-1958

Library Association[13]

Jast, Louis Stanley	1930-1931
Savage, Ernest A.	1936
Sayers, W. C. Berwick	1938
Esdaile, Arundell J. K.	1939-1945
Francis, Sir Frank C.	1965
Paulin, Lorna V.	1966

SUMMARY

An examination of the careers of our most frequently cited authors reveals that there are 56 which were at one time or another associated with just five institutions. These are: Columbia University, University of Chicago, Library of Congress, New York Public Library, and the University of Michigan.

Melvil Dewey, William W. Bishop, James C. M. Hanson, Louis R. Wilson, Andrew D. Osborn and Seymour Lubetzky are good examples of key figures in "invisible colleges." As was shown in Chapters V and VI, these individuals had *many* interrelationships with other catalogers. These contacts formed networks of numerous direct and indirect ties which constituted a chain of "invisible colleges."

The institutions with which so many of the authors in this study were associated had periods in which many of our most cited authors were there, and times when no one from this group was represented. The Library of Congress had many of these people at the turn of the century, but then from about 1915 to 1940 no one from this group went there. The Graduate Library School of the University of Chicago was established in 1928 and from that time until 1942 many of these authors were associated with the University of Chicago. The University of Michigan attracted several of these catalogers during the time that William Warner Bishop was the director of the Library and later head of the Library School. Bishop was there from 1915 until his retirement in 1941. During the 1920's and the 1930's many of these authors were also to be found in New York City at both the New York Public Library and Columbia University. After 1940 the Library of Congress began to employ a large share of these frequently cited authors, and our "national library" again asserted itself as the leading institution in the field of cataloging.

In 1951 an award was established to honor a highly respected cataloger and teacher, Margaret Mann, who, incidentally, is the fourth most highly cited person in this study (cf. Chapter III, Table 1). Since 1951, 13 of the catalogers mentioned in this study have been awarded the "Margaret Mann Citation in Cataloging and Classification." In order to illustrate that catalogers are also prominent in the entire profession of librarianship, and not just in the area of cataloging, 16 of the frequently cited persons in this study have been elected President of a national library association.

FOOTNOTES

1. Note: There is some overlap here because 34 (49.25%) of the 69 authors were associated with two or more of these institutions at different times.
2. Crane, Diana. *Invisible colleges; diffusion of knowledge in scientific communities*. Chicago, University of Chicago Press, 1972. p. 140.
3. Butler, Pierce. "James Christian Meinich Hanson," *Library quarterly*, 4:129, April 1934.
4. "University of Michigan courses in library science," *Library journal*, 51:565-566, June 15, 1926.

5. "Paris Library School," *A.L.A. bulletin*, 21:765-771, December 1927.

6. "Margaret Mann dies," *Library journal*, 85:3634, October 15, 1960.

7. "W. W. Bishop retires," *Library journal*, 66:564, June 15, 1941.

8. "Columbia University School of Library Service," *Library journal*, 51:476-477, June 15, 1926.

9. This award was established by the Division of Cataloging and Classification (now a Section of the Resources and Technical Services Division), American Library Association in 1950. cf. "The Margaret Mann award," *Journal of cataloging and classification*, 7:73, Summer 1951.

10. "Margaret Mann award winners, 1951-1966," *Library resources and technical services*, 11:24, Winter 1967. Angell, Richard S. "C. Sumner Spalding," *Library resources and technical services*, 12:67-69, Winter 1968. Carnovsky, Ruth French. "Paul S. Dunkin," *Library resources and technical services*, 12: 447-449, Fall 1968. Atherton, Pauline. "Dr. S. R. Ranganathan," *Library resources and technical services*, 14:582-584, Fall 1970.

11. Institute on Cataloging Code Revision, Stanford University, 1958. *Summary of proceedings*. Stanford, Calif., 1958. 62p.

Institute on Catalog Code Revision, McGill University, 1960. *Summary of proceedings*. Chicago, American Library Association, 1960. 93p.

International Conference on Cataloguing Principles, Paris, 1961. *Report*. London, International Federation of Library Associations, 1963. 293p.

12. American Library Association. *Membership directory, 1972*. Chicago, 1972. p. x-xi. Note: Linderfelt does not appear in the official list, but as explained earlier he *was* President for 6 months.

13. Munford, William A., ed. *Annals of the Library Association, 1877 to 1960*. London, The Library Association, 1965. 128p.

"Annual election, 1965," *Library Association record*, 66:588, December 1964.

"Annual election, 1966," *Library Association record*, 67:445, December 1965.

CHAPTER VIII

MISCELLANEOUS RELATIONSHIPS AMONG THE REMAINING MOST CITED AUTHORS

Interrelationships have thus far been established for 94 persons and there still remain 31 individuals to be accounted for, 7 Americans and 24 others. It was not possible to verify relationships among ten of the foreign librarians, and they will be discussed later in this chapter. But individual relationships among the 7 Americans and 14 of the Europeans were documented.

INTERRELATIONSHIPS AMONG THE REMAINING AMERICAN AND FOREIGN LIBRARIANS

The 21 persons who have not been mentioned heretofore will now be connected in some way with another person whose name has appeared previously. This group consists of seven Americans: Winona Adams, Emma Baldwin, Samuel Boggs, Bertha Buelow, Ralph Hagedorn, William Marcus, and Watson O'Dell Pierce. It also includes ten Britons: Denis Arnold, Stanley Butcher, Arthur Chaplin, Arundell Esdaile, Frank C. Francis, Leonard Jolley, Russell Mortimer, Lorna Paulin, Mary Piggott, and Arthur Wells; three Germans: Hermann Fuchs, Arnim Graesel, and Georg Schneider; and one Yugoslav: Eva Verona.

To begin at the earliest point in time, Arnim Graesel of the Universitäts-Bibliothek at Göttingen, almost certainly knew Karl Dziatzko, whose name has already been mentioned as attending the International Library Conference in London in 1897. They both attended a meeting together in 1902.[1]

There were just 25 persons at the fifth meeting of the Comité International des Bibliothèques in Berne in 1932. The American President of this meeting was William Warner Bishop, librarian at the University of Michigan, and the British Vice President, Arundell Esdaile of the British Museum. Hermann Fuchs from Germany also attended this meeting and, with only 25 in attendance, it is most unlikely that he could have avoided Bishop and Esdaile![2]
Fuchs and another of our personal authors, Georg Schneider, were both active members of Die Vereinigung Berliner Bibliothekare in the 1930's.[3]

In the same period, Bertha Buelow attended the meeting of the Catalog Section at the A.L.A. Conference in Denver in June 1935, and presented her paper on cataloging costs. Also present at that Section meeting were some of the authors from the "big ten" institutions: Arnold Trotier, Keyes D. Metcalf, Donald Coney and Rudolph Gjelsness.[4]

Dorothy Cornwell Lewis, who had attended the University of Illinois in 1928, went to work in 1930 in Washington at the Department of State's Division of Geography and Cartography. While there she was the co-author of a book with Samuel Whittemore Boggs. In the second page of its preface they state:

> Special acknowledgement is gratefully made of cooperation on the part of several specialists in the Library of Congress: . . . Mr. Charles Martel, Consultant in Cataloging; . . . Miss Mary Wilson MacNair; . . .[5]

Martel and MacNair, of course, are in the list of the 86 most cited authors (Chapter III, Table 1).

In 1940, Fremont Rider, who was a student in Dewey's Library School, was on the Advisory Committee to the "Committee for the Study of Cost Accounting in Public Libraries" of which William E. Marcus was the Chairman and Emma V. Baldwin, the Executive Secretary.[6]

The following year, Winona Adams read her paper at a meeting of the Pacific Northwest Library Association. Dorothy Alvord, who studied at Columbia University in 1919 and 1920, was present at that meeting in October 1942.[7]

Ralph Hagedorn went to the University of Wisconsin Library as head of the Acquisition Department in 1945.[8] George C. Allez, who received his library degree from Columbia University in 1929, was also at the University of Wisconsin Library.

In explaining the methods used in his study on work measurements, Watson O'Dell Pierce acknowledges in his "Notes on methods" that:

> Professor Maurice F. Tauber . . . , Columbia University, made available additional theses, surveys, and published material. . . . Miss Emma V. Baldwin and Mr. William E. Marcus discussed very fully their previous work on library measurement.[9]

Tauber is in the list of the 86 most cited authors (Chapter III, Table 1), while Baldwin and Marcus, as noted above, were acquainted with Fremont Rider.

A group of cited authors appeared as lecturers in a series given in March 1953 in a vacation course at the School of Librarianship and Archives of the University of London. Mary Piggott, a lecturer at this school, edited these talks and they were published as a collection. Those who gave lectures and wrote them up for publication are: Denis Arnold, Stanley Butcher, Leonard Jolley, Russell Mortimer, Lorna Paulin, and Arthur Wells.[10] Some may have met personally at this time if they did not already know each other. Others, such as Jolley and Wells, were probably already acquainted through their mutual interest in classification. Jolley and Wells were also two of the 20 persons listed as active members of the Classification Research Group.[11]

Finally, of the 105 participants at the 1961 International Conference on Cataloguing Principles held in Paris, there are 13 (8 American and 5 foreign catalogers) who appear in our list of 125 most frequently cited authors: viz., Richard Angell, Arthur Chaplin, Paul Dunkin, Werner Ellinger, Frank Francis, Cloyd Dake Gull, Seymour Lubetzky, Andrew Osborn, Mary Piggott,

S. R. Ranganathan, C. Sumner Spalding, Eva Verona, and Wyllis Wright.[12] The differences of opinion between Lubetzky and Verona are well known.[13]

Sir Frank Francis and Arthur Chaplin were both at the British Museum for at least forty years. Francis, the Director and Principal Librarian, was there from 1926 until his retirement in 1968.[14] Chaplin started at the British Museum in 1930, he became Principal Keeper of Printed Books in 1966, and retired in 1970.[15] Both of these men surely knew Arundell Esdaile who was at the British Museum from 1903 until his retirement in 1940.[16]

Chaplin delivered a paper at the twenty-first annual conference of the Graduate Library School of the University of Chicago held in June 1956. Others who presented papers at that conference were: Ruth French Strout, Andrew Osborn, Paul Dunkin, Raynard Swank, Richard Angell, Wyllis Wright, Herman Henkle, Benjamin Custer and Seymour Lubetzky.[17] Everyone who delivered a paper at that conference appears among our most cited authors! Chaplin was awarded the Margaret Mann Citation in Cataloging and Classification in 1963; he was the first non-American to receive this award.[18]

EUROPEANS FOR WHOM NO RELATIONSHIPS WERE DETERMINED

It was hypothesized that there exist opportunities and probabilities for some sort of a continuous chain of personal contact among all 125 persons being studied. The possibilities for personal contact have been established for all but 10 of the 125. These ten are all Europeans. It is very likely that the inability to establish the possible circumstances for personal contact between the 10 (8%) and the other 115 (92%) is due to the unavailability of full biographical data and not because there were no contacts. The ten are: Dorothy May Norris (British); Giuseppe Fumagalli (Italian); Leopold Hesse, Albert Maire and Edouard Rouveyre (French); and Walter Bauhuis, Wilhelm Frels, Rudolf Kaiser, Adolf Keysser and Hermann Mecklenburg (German).

The only Briton not linked to anyone else was Dorothy May Norris, still living, and as far as can be determined she is still at her post in the Birmingham Reference Library, where she has spent her entire professional career.[19]

The Italian, Giuseppe Fumagalli, was librarian at the Biblioteca Vittorio Emanuale in Rome at the time he published his book in 1887. He died in 1937.

Of the three French authors, Leopold Hesse was a contemporary of Panizzi, but no opportunity for contact could be found. Hesse wrote under the pseudonym of "Constantin." His *Bibliothéconomie* was published in 1841, the same year that Panizzi's "91 rules" appeared.

Albert Maire and Edouard Rouveyre lived and published in Paris at the same time, that is, in the last quarter of the nineteenth century. Maire was the "Sous-Bibliothecarie" at the Sorbonne and Rouveyre was "Officier de l'Instruction Publique" in Paris, according to the title pages of their books. It is quite likely that they knew Leopold Delisle, as well as each other, but this could not be documented.

Even though it is very likely that the four Germans who were born in the nineteenth century, Wilhelm Frels, Rudolf Kaiser, Adolf Keysser and Hermann Mecklenburg, were acquainted with each other and probably knew Graesel and Dziatzko, nothing to document this could be found. Frels almost certainly knew Kaiser because in the "Vorwort" of his book he states that Kaiser supplied him with important materials for his text.[20]

Hermann Mecklenburg and Rudolf Kaiser were both at the Königliche Bibliothek, but Kaiser went there two years after Mecklenburg died at the early age of 39. Adolf Keysser was librarian at the Kölner Stadtbibliothek, and it is quite possible that he may have known Kaiser; both were very active in professional affairs at the same time.

The other German, Walter Bauhuis, was born in 1905 and even though it is unlikely that he knew any of these other Germans, he may very well have known some of his American or British contemporaries.

SUMMARY

In larger view, the United States and Great Britain emerge as the two leading countries in cataloging, at least in numbers and in the time span covered by the authors. Beginning with Panizzi and Jewett, there has been a continuous chain of Americans and Britons active in cataloging. The Germans, the French and the one Italian mentioned here were all active during a much shorter span of time: an approximate period from 1875 to 1925. But at no time did the activity of the Germans and French ever surpass that of their English speaking colleagues. A surprising 92% of cited authors turned out to be acquainted with each other to a greater or lesser degree. Only 8% (ten persons) appear to have operated in limbo, and probably this figure could be cut if full biographical data were available for this study.

FOOTNOTES

1. "Verein deutscher Bibliothekare," *Zentralblatt für Bibliothekswesen*, 19:369, August 1902.
2. International Federation of Library Associations, *Actes du Comité International des Bibliothèques*. 5me session, Berne, 1932. La Haye, Martinus Nijhoff, 1932. pp. 3-4.
3. "Umschau aus und über Bibliotheken," *Zentralblatt für Bibliothekswesen*, 50:490, Juli 1933.

"Umschau aus und über Bibliotheken," *Zentralblatt für Bibliothekswesen*, 54:359, Juli 1937.
4. Buelow, Bertha Elizabeth. "Cataloging costs," *Library journal*, 60:657, September 1, 1935.

"Catalog Section," *A.L.A. bulletin*, 29:589-598, September 1935.
5. Boggs, Samuel W. and Dorothy C. Lewis. *The classification and cataloging of maps and atlases*. New York, Special Libraries Association, 1945. 175p.

6. Baldwin, Emma V. and William E. Marcus. *Library costs and budgets; a study of cost accounting in public libraries.* New York, Bowker, 1941. p. 159.

7. Adams, Winona Josephine. "A divided catalog in practice," *PNLA quarterly*, 7:48-50, October 1942.

"P.N.L.A. membership list," *PNLA quarterly*, 7:105 and 107, October 1942.

8. "Appointments, etc.," *Library journal*, 70:590, June 15, 1945.

9. Pierce, Watson O'Dell. *Work measurement in public libraries.* New York, Social Science Research Council, 1949. Appendix D. p. 236.

10. Piggott, Mary, ed. *Cataloguing principles and practice; an inquiry.* London, The Library Association, 1954. pp. v-viii.

11. Classification Research Group. "Bulletin no. 8," *Journal of documentation*, 20:165, September 1964.

12. International Conference on Cataloguing Principles, Paris, 1961. *Report*. London, International Federation of Library Associations, 1963. pp. 1-6.

13. Ball, Katharine. "The Paris conference," *Library resources and technical services*, 6:172-175, Spring 1962.

14. "People," *Library journal*, 93:2961, September 1, 1968.

15. "People," *Library journal*, 95:1699, May 1, 1970.

16. "Retirement of Dr. Esdaile from the British Museum," *Library Association record*, 42:107, April 1940.

17. Strout, Ruth French, ed. *Toward a better cataloging code.* Chicago, University of Chicago Press, 1957. 116p.

18. Ball, Katharine L. "Arthur Hugh Chaplin," *Library resources and technical services*, 7:309-311, Fall 1963.

19. Landau, Thomas, ed. *Who's who in librarianship.* p. 150.

20. Frels, Wilhelm. *Die bibliothekarische Titelaufnahme in Deutschland.* Leipzig, Harrassowitz, 1919, p. v.

CHAPTER IX

THE TIME DIMENSION OF THE MOST FREQUENTLY CITED WORKS

A purely quantitative analysis of the number of times that a given work is cited should not be construed as an indication of its true value. In conjunction with the number of times that a given work is cited it is necessary to analyze the age of the work each time it is cited. Many works are frequently cited during a short span of time immediately following publication. This may indicate that they are widely read, and that they have made an impact, but on the other hand, after a few years they may never be referred to again. If this be the case then such works must be considered as ephemeral and in no way qualify to be deemed "classics." However, works that stand the test of time in terms of "citation duration" rather than "citation frequency," that is, citation over a long period of time merit the appellation of "classic." For any given writing there are an infinitesimal number of patterns that the citations could follow. The results of various studies point out that very few writings (journal articles as well as monographs) are cited after they reach the age of 20 years.[1] Derek Price calculated that those scientific papers which are still being frequently cited 20 or more years after their publication probably account for less than 1% of the total production in any given subject.[2] He also estimated that only 1% of all *scientific* papers are ever cited more than six times.[3]

If this be the case, then the quantitative factor of being cited six or more times (citation frequency) in addition to the time dimension of an age older than 20 years at time of citation (citation duration) would seem to establish the minimum threshold over which a scientific work would have to pass in order to qualify as a classic. Derek Price went on to hypothesize that:

> ... results to date could be explained by the hypothesis that every year about 10 percent of all papers "die" not to be cited again, and that for the "live" papers the chance of being cited at least once in any year is about 60 percent. This would mean that the major work of a *paper* would be finished after 10 years. The process thus reaches a steady state, in which about 10 percent of all published papers have never been cited, about 10 percent have been cited once, about 9 percent twice, and so on, the percentages slowly decreasing, so that half of all papers will be cited eventually five times or more and a quarter of all papers, ten times or more. More work is urgently needed on the problem of determining whether there is a probability that the more a paper is cited the more likely it is to be cited thereafter. It seems to me that further work in this area might well lead to the

discovery that classic papers could be rapidly identified, and that perhaps even the "superclassics" would prove so distinctive that they could be picked automatically by means of citation-index-production procedures and published as a single *U.S. (or World) Journal of Really Important Papers.*[4]

It should be noted that Price is referring to the type of science where research results are cumulative and where each generation builds on the work of the previous ones. In cataloging, this is not exactly the same. Seymour Lubetzky, for example, in the 1950's went back over a century to the work of Panizzi in his attempt to bring some logic into the development of cataloging rules. Cataloging brings greater resemblance to patterns in non-cumulative research, about which, as yet, there has been very little quantitative study. At this time it is not known whether the scientific journal citation patterns hold for non-scientific fields, especially those where the monograph is the principal vehicle for research publication. However, it should be mentioned that the age of the citations reported in the studies listed at the beginning of this chapter do concur with Derek Price's idea that "the major work of a paper would be finished after 10 years."[5]

The aforementioned studies on citation patterns used previously defined bodies of literature and analyzed their references and the works cited. (These bodies of literature were often made up entirely of journal articles, but several studies used monographs and serial publications, while others were based solely on monographs.) In contrast, the investigation being detailed here began with a single work in book form from which a body of writings, consisting almost equally of monographs and articles, was created by identifying a network through citations, therefore only cited writings appear in the network. The number of works never cited cannot be determined, nor can it be ascertained how many times each of the 184 works has been cited outside of this network. This brings up some interesting questions: Are these most frequently cited works the same as those that have been cited most often in the entire body of literature on cataloging? Would Cutter's *Rules for a dictionary catalog* remain the most cited work? Would the rank and order according to the number of times cited remain the same for the 184 works if a citation analysis for *all* works on cataloging were studied, rather than the network which was identified in this study? This is an area still requiring further research.

Extrapolating from the findings of several discrete studies in many fields, it seems fairly safe to make the hypothesis that works which are more than 20 years old, and still frequently cited, can be called "classics." If works which are heavily cited for 20 years can be considered as "classics," and those few which are cited over a much longer period of years can be termed "superclassics," then this study has discovered a number of works which fall into these categories. However, for this study it was decided that a longer period of time was needed, so that only those writings with a citation frequency of 15 or more and a minimum citation duration of 50 years would be called classics.

In the entire study, the 184 works which were cited 8 times or more each have a total of 2,917 citations. There are 58 of the 184 works which were cited

15 or more times; these 58 works account for 1,642 of the 2,917 citations. In other words, 31% of the most cited works received 56% of the citations.

There are five works which were cited more than 50 times. These are: Charles A. Cutter's *Rules for a dictionary catalog* which was cited 138 times; the American Library Association's *Catalog rules* of 1908 was cited 96 times; Margaret Mann's *Introduction to cataloging and the classification of books* had 81 citations; the *A.L.A. cataloging rules for author and title entries* published by the American Library Association in 1949 was cited 65 times; and Seymour Lubetzky's *Cataloging rules and principles* which was cited 54 times.

Table 13 gives the other 53 works which were cited 15 or more times in order of their citation frequency. They are grouped according to the number of citations each received. Only the last name of the author is given along with the reference number to the listing in Appendix I. For the exact number of times each was cited and for complete bibliographical data it is necessary to consult Appendix I.

TABLE 13
Works Cited 15 or More Times in Order of Citation Frequency

40-49 Citations
  Vatican Library (173); Osborn (135); Fellows (55); Bishop (18).

30-39 Citations
  Jewett (86); Prussian instructions (144); Akers (2); Sharp (161); Hitchler (80); Library of Congress (98).

20-29 Citations
  British Museum (25); Quinn (145); American Library Association (7); MacPherson (111); Taube (168); Mudge (124); Pierson (142); Linderfelt (102); Ranganathan (149); Hanson (68); Wheatley (179); Fletcher (58); Graesel (64); Hanson (69); Italy (84); Pettee (139); Ranganathan (151).

15-19 Citations
  Chaplin (32); Rider (154); Rider (156); Ver Nooy (174); Allez (5); Brown (27); Dean (43); Frels (60); Kaiser (94); Lubetzky (105); MacNair (110); American Library Association (10); British Museum (24); Childs (34); Dewey (46); Wright (182); American Library Association (11); Cutter (40); Dunkin (48); Lubetzky (103); Nyholm (129); Panizzi (136); Ranganathan (152); Rider (155); Swank (167); Tauber (170).

Table 14 gives the 58 works in order of their citation duration. Part A of Table 14 lists the 14 works with a citation duration of more than 50 years, which are considered to be classics and superclassics. Included with each work are the times cited, the span of years in which it was cited, and the citation duration. Part B of Table 14 groups the remaining 44 works into 10 year periods according to the citation duration of each work. Following the same pattern as Table 13 only the last name is given along with the reference number to the listing in Appendix I.

TABLE 14

Works Cited 15 or More Times in Order of Citation Duration

Part A—Works with a citation duration of more than fifty years

	Author and Title	Times Cited	Period of Citations	Duration in Years
1.	British Museum Report of the Commissioners...	16	1852-1969	118
2.	Cutter, Charles A. Rules for a dictionary catalog	138	1885-1969	85
3.	Panizzi, Sir Anthony Rules for the compilation of the catalogue	15	1885-1963	79
4.	Cutter, Charles A. Library catalogues	15	1887-1964	78
5.	Jewett, Charles Coffin On the construction of catalogues of libraries...	38	1887-1964	78
6.	Wheatley, Henry Benjamin How to catalogue a library	22	1890-1967	78
7.	Dewey, Melvil Library school rules	16	1897-1963	67
8.	Linderfelt, Klas August Eclectic card catalog rules	23	1902-1963	62
9.	American Library Association Condensed rules for an author and title catalog	16	1903-1963	61
10.	Graesel, Arnim Handbuch der Bibliothekslehre	20	1896-1956	61
11.	American Library Association Catalog rules (1908)	96	1908-1967	60

TABLE 14 (cont'd)

	Author and Title	Times Cited	Period of Citations	Duration in Years
12.	British Museum Rules for compiling the catalogues...	29	1904-1961	58
13.	Quinn, John Henry Library cataloguing	28	1903-1959	57
14.	Prussian instructions	38	1914-1964	51

Part B—Works with a citation duration of less than fifty years

40-49 Years
Fletcher (58); Hitchler (80); Kaiser (94); Frels (60); Fellows (55); Brown (27).

30-39 Years
Italy (84); Bishop (18); MacNair (110); Akers (2); Sharp (161); Mann (113); Pettee (139); American Library Association (11); Childs (34); Ranganathan (149); Vatican Library (173).

20-29 Years
Hanson (69); Mudge (124); Osborn (135); Pierson (142); American Library Association (7); Rider (156); MacPherson (111); Nyholm (129); Hanson (68); Rider (154); Allez (5); Ranganathan (152); American Library Association (8); Dean (43); Wright (182); Library of Congress (98); Ver Nooy (174).

9-19 Years
Rider (155); Taube (168); Lubetzky (104); Lubetzky (103); Chaplin (32); Dunkin (48); Ranganathan (148); Swank (167); Tauber (170); Lubetzky (105).

The 58 works listed in Tables 13 and 14 have been classified into nine groups. Three discrete criteria were used in their classification: the citation duration, the aspect of cataloging treated, and the type of prediction that could be made collectively for the group. The nine groups are: superclassics, classics, cataloging codes, works on corporate entry, cataloging manuals, writings on library catalogs, theoretical and historical treatises, works which are dying, and those which are too new to allow prediction of their future value.

The works in Table 14 which had a citation duration of more than 50 years are considered to be "classics" in the field of cataloging; of the 14 works which fall into this category there are 6 which have a citation duration of more than 75 years and are deemed "superclassics."

In order to study the citation pattern of each of the 58 works listed in Tables 13 and 14 the date of each citation was recorded in chronological order. These were then grouped into five year periods, beginning with the year of publication of the first cited edition or version. The number of times cited in each five year period was converted to a percentage, and a bar graph was made for each work. The graphs facilitated the task of determining the extent to which each work was cited during every five year period of its history, i.e., from the year of publication until 1969. The results of the analyses of the graphs are discussed below.

In the text that follows the titles of journal articles are placed between quotation marks, and the titles of books and contributions to monographs are in italics. Thus it is easy to distinguish which are books and which are articles.

SUPERCLASSICS

The first group consisting of six works are herein called "superclassics"; they all have a citation duration of no less than 75 years, the range being from 78 to 118 years. These six were all published between 1841 and 1889.

The oldest two of these "superclassics" are both works emanating from the British Museum, Panizzi's *Rules. . .* (1841) and the *Report of the Commissioners. . .* (1850). The British Museum *Report of the Commissioners. . .* has the longest citation duration of the 58 works being discussed here, and it was 100 years old when it was cited most heavily. During the nineteenth century it was only cited sporadically, but in the twentieth century it was always cited just before a new cataloging code appeared, that is, prior to the years 1908, 1941, 1949, and 1967. The most heavily cited period in its history was in the two decades preceding the publication of the Anglo-American cataloging rules in 1967.

Panizzi's *Rules for the compilation of the catalogue* and Jewett's *On the construction of catalogues. . .* are the oldest cataloging codes that appeared in this study. They were published just 11 years apart, and their "citation histories" are surprisingly similar. Neither was cited until the 1880's. Hermann Mecklenburg, a German librarian, cited Panizzi in 1885 and then Giuseppe Fumagalli, an Italian, cited both Panizzi and Jewett in his book on cataloging which was published in 1887. Both seem to have been forgotten for at least 35 years before someone made reference to their work. Their citation patterns seem to peak and fall approximately in the same periods. Both were most heavily cited in the 20 year period from 1946 to 1966; this is almost 100 years after their publication. Centenarian works which are still being cited most surely deserve to be called "superclassics."

Charles Cutter's importance and impact on this field are made even more evident when it is revealed that he is the author of *two* superclassics: *Library catalogues* and *Rules for a dictionary catalog*. Surprisingly, both first appeared in 1876 in the Bureau of Education's report, *Public libraries in the United States of America; their history, condition, and management*. The most frequently cited work of the entire study was Cutter's *Rules for a dictionary catalog*. After its first citation in the 1880's it has been continuously referred to by writers. Undoubtedly this work has had an impact on all cataloging codes since the publication of the first edition in 1876. Cutter's work on library catalogs has not been cited as frequently as his code of cataloging rules, but its citation duration is almost as extensive.

The remaining superclassic is the second edition of Wheatley's *How to catalogue a library*; the first edition never appeared in the network. The second edition was published in 1889, and has been continuously cited throughout its 80 year history.

CLASSICS

The next group consists of eight works which are considered to be "classics," since each has a citation duration of at least 50 years. Six of these eight are cataloging codes and were all published within a period of 25 years (1883-1908).

The oldest and youngest of these six codes, the *Condensed rules...* and the *Catalog rules*, were both produced by the American Library Association. The *Condensed rules* served as the basis for the *Catalog rules* of 1908. In contrast to the continuous referral to Cutter's *Rules* and the "1908 code," the *Condensed rules* seem only to be used at the time when a catalog revision is underway. This phenomenon seems to be shared by all codes. The only exception being that for some unknown reason the *Condensed rules* was cited just *before* the 1941 preliminary edition of the A.L.A. cataloging code, but it does not appear to have been cited for the 1949 edition. However, this work was again used heavily in those years just before the publication of the Anglo-American cataloging rules of 1967.

The *Catalog rules* of 1908 is the second most frequently cited work in this study, and like Cutter's *Rules for a dictionary catalog* its citations have been continuous since its publication. However, its use seems to have reached its apex in the 1930's and since then it has gradually tapered off.

The next four works are also cataloging codes and were published between 1890 and 1900; the British Museum's *Rules* first came out in 1900; Dewey's *Library school rules* appeared in several editions between 1892 and 1905; Linderfelt's *Eclectic card catalog rules* came out in 1890; and the *Prussian instructions* first came out in 1899.

Table 11 in Chapter IV pointed out the two periods in which the majority of the most cited works were published: the 1930's and the 1950's. These are exactly the same periods in which most of the works were also most heavily cited. Cutter's *Rules for a dictionary catalog*, Wheatley's *How to catalogue a library*, the *Catalog rules* of 1908, the British Museum's *Rules for compiling the catalogues...*, Dewey's *Library school rules*, and Linderfelt's *Eclectic card catalog rules* were all most heavily cited during the 1930's. One reason that the *Prussian instructions* was not cited as heavily during the 1930's as the other codes is that it is the only one which was not originally published in English; the English translation did not appear until 1938.

The other two "classics" are Graesel's *Handbuch der Bibliothekslehre* and Quinn's *Library cataloguing*. Graesel's *Handbuch* is unique in that it is the only classic that has never been available in English. It was published in French in 1897, and in Spanish in 1914. This *Handbuch* reached its "popular era" in the decade 1932-1942, which is more than 40 years after its original publication date. The other classic, Quinn's *Library cataloguing*, has appeared in two editions, in 1899 and 1913. It was often cited in the 1930's, but since then it has been cited just three times. This leads one to suspect that it is dying.

CATALOGING CODES

This group consists of six books of cataloging rules. They may be called potential classics due to the number of citations each has received and the age at the time of being cited. Three of these are foreign: two are Italian, the Vatican Library's *Rules for the catalog of printed books* and the *Regole per la compilazione del catalogo alfabetico* published by Italy's Direzione generale delle accademie e biblioteche; the other one from India is Ranganathan's *Classified catalogue code*. The Italian government code has come out in three editions in 1922, 1932, and 1958. Except for the period of World War II, it has been consistently cited. However, it should be noted that the periods in which it was most heavily cited all follow immediately after the appearance of a new edition.

The rules of the Vatican Library have been continuously cited since the first edition came out in 1931. The second and third editions in Italian came out in 1939 and 1949. The Spanish translation came out in 1940 and the Portuguese one in 1949. The English version appeared in 1948 and it was in the following decade that its citations reached an all-time high.

Ranganathan's *Classified catalogue code* has appeared in four editions: 1934, 1945, 1952, and 1958. The analysis of the dates in which this work was cited seemed to indicate that if he had not written a second edition, the work might have died because shortly after the second edition appeared it came to life and as each succeeding edition appeared the citations increased. This brings up an interesting question: Is the fourth edition strong enough to become a "classic" without any further revisions now that Ranganathan has died? It is a potential classic according to the standards previously defined, but will it make the grade?

The three American works, the 1941 and the 1949 cataloging codes published by the American Library Association, and the Library of Congress' *Rules for descriptive cataloging*, were all published in the 1940's. All three were often referred to in the years prior to the publication of the 1967 Anglo-American code and it is highly likely that in the decade previous to the publication of the next new code that these will probably be heavily relied upon again. It should be noted that only three works were cited more times than the 1949 cataloging code, which was cited a total of 65 times in a period of less than 20 years.

CORPORATE ENTRY

Among these 58 frequently cited works there are two that deal specifically with corporate entry, Hanson's "Corporate authorship versus title entry" and Childs' *Author entry for government publications*. Both first appeared in 1935 and were cited last in 1964. Childs' work has been more steadily cited than Hanson's article, but both peaked in the 1950's.

CATALOGING MANUALS

Six of the eight cataloging manuals discussed here are among the 14 most cited works of the entire study (see Table 13). The most cited one is Margaret Mann's introductory text, which was cited 81 times, and is the third most often cited work in the entire study. The others are (in order of citation frequency): Dorcas Fellows' *Cataloging rules* with 43 citations; Bishop's *Practical handbook...* which was cited 40 times; Akers' *Simple library cataloging*, and Sharp's *Cataloging*, each with 37 citations; and Hitchler's *Cataloging for small libraries*, which was cited 35 times. The remaining two were much less frequently cited. James Duff Brown's *Manual of library economy* had just 17 citations. (Also this is the only one of the eight which is not exclusively a cataloging manual, but rather a general text on library science.) The other manual is Ranganathan's *Theory of library catalogue*, which was cited 15 times.

For historical continuity, the following discussion is chronological according to the date of the first edition of the eight cataloging manuals.

Brown's *Manual of library economy* has come out in seven editions. Only the first two editions (1903 and 1907) were Brown's alone. After his death in 1914, Berwick Sayers updated and brought out four later editions in 1920, 1931, 1937, and 1950. Sayers died in 1961 and in that same year Reginald Northwood Lock brought out the seventh edition of Brown's *Manual*. This manual was most heavily cited in the 1930's, but in the last 20 years it has not been cited at all. If this work is not already dead (as far as cataloging is concerned) it most certainly is moribund.

Theresa Hitchler was head cataloger at the Brooklyn Public Library when she published the three editions of her cataloging manual which came out in 1905, 1915, and 1926. It seems to have been very popular and was frequently cited. According to the dates of the citations it would appear that her first two editions were not as widely used as was the third. This work reached its apex in citations during the decade following the publication of the third edition. Since then it seems to have died; it has not been cited for two decades.

The first editions of the manuals of Dorcas Fellows and William Bishop both appeared in 1914. Strangely enough, Bishop's *first* edition had no citation until after the publication of the *second* edition in 1924. Fellows' second edition came out in 1922, while she was still teaching at the Library School in Albany. These two works have almost identical citation patterns, and, in fact, almost the same number of citations: Fellows had 43 and Bishop 40. Both appear to be losing momentum.

The citation patterns for the manuals of Akers and Mann indicate that perhaps both have had their heydays. It should be pointed out that Mann's work came out in only two editions, 1930 and 1943, while Akers published four editions in 1927, 1933, 1944, and 1954. (The fifth edition of Akers' manual did not appear until 1969, and therefore was too new to be cited in the network identified in this study.) In spite of the new editions, the number of citations for Akers' manual has been declining even faster than Mann's introductory text. Yet no new edition of Mann's work has appeared since 1943!

A comparison of the dates of the citations for Hitchler's cataloging manual with those of Akers and Mann shows that Hitchler was often cited until Akers and Mann published their manuals. Akers' first edition came out in 1927 and Mann's in 1930. An analysis of the citation patterns of these three works clearly indicates that the manuals of Akers and Mann superseded that of Hitchler.

Besides Brown's *Manual of library economy*, Sharp's *Cataloguing* is the only other English manual in this group. It was first published in 1935. The succeeding editions came out in 1937, 1944, and 1948. Even though the first edition appeared five years later than did that of Mann, and Sharp brought out three later editions and Mann only one, the citation pattern of Sharp is not unlike that of Mann's text. Also, the total number of citations for Sharp's work is only 37, as compared to the 81 for Mann. Almost 70 percent of Sharp's citations were in the same fifteen year period in which the four editions appeared, 1935-1948. Since then it has been cited less and less, although the most recent citations (1965-1969) are to Sharp and not to Mann. The citation patterns of Sharp's book and that of Mann are surprisingly similar.

The last manual in this group is that of Ranganathan. His *Theory of library catalogue* was first published in 1938 and since then it was only cited 15 times in 22 years. In this group of eight works Ranganathan's *Theory of library catalogue* is the only one which never had a second edition.

It can be said from the foregoing data that Mann's *Introduction to cataloging and the classification of books* is not only the most cited *manual*, but also one cited as much as others which have had more recent revised editions. One might deduce from this that even though there are more recent texts than that of Mann, hers has proven its superiority through its quality. It has stood the test of both citation frequency and citation duration.

LIBRARY CATALOGS

In the group of 58 works which were cited 15 or more times, there appear eight writings concerning the catalog. One of these, Cutter's *Library catalogues*, was considered as a superclassic and discussed earlier. Fletcher's "Future of the catalog" is the oldest of the remaining seven articles on the catalog. It was first published in the *Library journal* in 1905. Its citation duration of 49 years is only one year short of being considered a classic according to the standards established earlier in this chapter. Even though it has had continuous use since its publication, it was used most frequently *after* it was 35 years old.

Three of the other six writings deal with the divided catalog: Allez's "In defence of the alphabetical catalog," Dean's "Shall we divide our catalog vertically?," and Nyholm's "California divides its catalog." The other three treat the problem of the large and ever-growing dictionary catalogs: two are by Rider, *Alternatives for the present dictionary catalog* and "The possibility of discarding the card catalog"; the other is Wright's "Horizontal division of the catalog."

These six all happen to have been written from 1938 to 1940, and were cited from 15 to 19 times each during the next 25 years. Even though they were often cited in the 15 years following their publication (the range is from 68% to 83% during that period) they were all still being cited after 20 years, indicating that they appear to be good candidates for consideration as classics someday. The next two or three decades should determine their lasting value.

THEORETICAL AND HISTORICAL TREATISES

The six works treated under this broad heading fall into two discrete groups according to their citation duration. The four American works: Hanson's *A comparative study of cataloging rules...*, Pettee's "The development of authorship entry...," Osborn's "The crisis in cataloging," and Mudge's "Present day economies in cataloging" were written between 1934 and 1941 and the span of their citation duration is 25 to 32 years. The other two works are German: Frel's *Die bibliothekarische Titelaufnahme in Deutschland* and Kaiser's "Vergleichung der englisch-amerikanischen Katalogregeln..."; the citation duration for Frels is 44 years and that for Kaiser is 46 years.

The works by Hanson and Pettee both were most heavily cited in the late 1950's, which is about 20 years after their publication. Pettee was cited 20 times in the network and Hanson 22 times. The articles by Osborn and Mudge both have a citation duration of 29 years and were most often cited at the beginning of the 1940's, which is immediately after they were written. Mudge had a citation frequency of 24 and Osborn was cited 45 times, which makes the latter rank seventh among the most frequently cited writings. All four have continued to be cited relatively often in the past 20 years and if the trend continues they may well be on their way to becoming classics.

The two German works by Frels and Kaiser were both written in the same decade and their citation patterns are quite similar. Both were most heavily cited in the 1950's and even though they have a fairly continuous pattern, neither was cited during World War II. Each has been cited exactly 17 times in the network. The high citation duration and the low citation frequency may be due in part to the fact that neither was ever translated into English.

MORIBUND WORKS

The seven works grouped here as moribund do not seem to have been cited during the past decade or cited only once. All appear to have outlived their usefulness. MacPherson's book is a perfect example of a work which is heavily cited in the first few years after its publication and then gradually tapers off. Ver Nooy's article was cited for the first 15 years and then seems to have been forgotten. The same pattern holds for Rider's "Library cost accounting" and Swank's article on the cataloging department. The guides to cataloging serials by MacNair and Pierson were published at about the same time. The first edition of MacNair's guide came out in 1918, but was not cited until after the publication of the second edition in 1920. The third edition was published in 1925. Pierson's guide was first published in 1919, and was only cited once prior to the publication of the second edition in 1931. Their citation patterns are quite similar, both were most heavily cited from 1928 to 1932 and neither was cited after 1959. (Incidentally, the professional careers of these two first cousins were even more similar than the citation patterns of their serials cataloging guides.) The A.L.A. survey was most frequently cited within the first ten years and since then has been slowly declining.

WORKS TOO NEW FOR PREDICTION

The final eight works, which were classified as too new to determine their value, were all published between 1950 and 1960. However, the number of citations runs the gamut from the minimum of 15 up to 54 citations. The most cited *author* of the entire study, Seymour Lubetzky, wrote three of the eight works. His *Cataloging rules and principles* has been cited 54 times and ranks fifth in the total number of citations for a single *work* (see page 66). This work may well prove to be a classic, but it is too soon to say for sure.

Tauber's book on technical services was cited only 15 times in as many years. This could indicate a dying work, and it may well be that the only remedy for this work would be a new edition. This remedy seems to have revived other dying works such as Brown's library manual and Hitchler's cataloging manual.

The remaining six works: Taube's article on the cataloging of publications of corporate authors, Lubetzky's rejoinder to this article by Taube, Ranganathan's *Heading and canons*, Chaplin's *Reconsideration of the British Museum rules. . .* , Lubetzky's cataloging code, and Dunkin's "Criticisms of current cataloging" are all no more than 20 years old and it is just too soon to even attempt to predict their chances of becoming classics.

SUMMARY

In view of the fact that so many previous citation studies have demonstrated that only a small percentage of works are ever cited after they are ten years old, there is little doubt that this study has identified some classics in the field of cataloging. The time dimension, in conjunction with the number of citations, points out some works which truly can be called "classics" and "superclassics."

Of the 58 works just analyzed, only 14 were considered classics and just 6 of these were called superclassics. Of the others, there are several which are definitely potential classics. Based on their citation duration and frequency, some of the most probable candidates are: Mann's *Introduction to cataloging and the classification of books*, Fletcher's "The future of the catalog," Osborn's "The crisis in cataloging," Pettee's "The development of authorship entry. . ." and Lubetzky's *Cataloging rules and principles*. There are others which may turn out to be classics also, but more time is needed to judge the fate of all of them.

FOOTNOTES

1. Broadus, Robert N. "The literature of the social sciences: a survey of citation studies," *International social science journal*, 23:236-243, 1971.

    Earle, Penelope and Brian Vickery. "Social science literature use in the UK as indicated by citations," *Journal of documentation*, 25:123-141, June 1969.

    Kessler, Maxwell Mirton. "Technical information flow patterns." In: Western Joint Computer Conference, Los Angeles, 1961. *Proceedings*. Los Angeles, National Joint Computer Committee, 1961. pp. 247-257.

    Lin, Nan and Carnot E. Nelson. "Bibliographic patterns in core sociological journals, 1965-1966," *American sociologist*, 4:47-50, February 1969.

    Xhignesse, Louis V. and Charles E. Osgood. "Bibliographical citation characteristics of the psychological journal network in 1950 and in 1960," *American psychologist*, 22: 778-791, September 1967.

    Weiss, Paul. "Knowledge: a growth process," *Science*, 131:1716-1719, June 10, 1960.
2. Price, Derek. "Networks of scientific papers." p. 513.
3. *Ibid.*, p. 511.
4. *Ibid.*, pp. 511-512.
5. *Ibid.*, p. 512.

CHAPTER X

CONCLUSIONS
Part 1—Results

THE INVESTIGATION

As stated in the introduction to this study, an attempt was made to identify a core literature in cataloging by creating a network of cited writings, beginning with the references in a single book, James Tait's *Authors and titles*, published in 1969. Each of the writings cited was looked up. The writings cited in the looked-up item was recorded and then these references in turn were also located. Thus a chain of citations was created and carried back to 1835, the year selected as a reasonable cut-off date. This procedure was followed for each of Tait's citations and their citations, and *their* citations, until either no further citation was possible or 1835 was reached. This made a fan-like network of overlapping citations based on all citations of works in the defined subject area. The forward cut-off date was 1969, the publication date of Tait's book. Previous citation studies have used a pre-established body of literature, but in this investigation a finite network was created from the references only, and covering a period of 135 years.

Tait's *Authors and titles* proved to be a good key for opening up and discovering the vast network of writings of and about cataloging. The total network consisted of 7,209 citations of 2,532 works by 1,412 authors, both personal and corporate. Of the 2,532 works, there were 184 which were cited eight or more times each. These 184 works and their 132 authors served as the basic data for the principal elements of this study. The 184 "most cited works" were grouped according to their similarities and a classification schedule of 15 categories was created quite easily, bearing out the contention of Robert A. Fairthorne that a viable classification could be made from such a fan-like network of citations. The two most heavily cited types of works were those classed as "cataloging codes" and "cataloging manuals."

THE AUTHORS

There were 86 authors whose works were cited 3,614 times in the network, in other words, less than 7% of the authors were responsible for 50.12% of the total number of citations. Such a Bradfordian distribution is similar to patterns in other literatures. These authors were cited at least 15 times each, and ten were cited more than 100 times each.

An analysis of the 132 authors of the 184 most cited works indicated that 82 (61.5%) were men, 34 (26.5%) were women, and the remaining 16 (12%) were corporate bodies. Of the 132 personal and corporate authors, 82 (62%) were Americans and wrote 124 (67%) of the 184 works; and 25 (20%) were British and produced 30 (17%) of the works. Due to these combined forces (82% of the authors), and others who also wrote in English, 160 (87%) of the works were originally written in English. Thus English was the most important language in cataloging throughout the entire 135 year period under consideration here. German ranked as the second language, although there were only 12 works (6.5%) of this group which were originally published in German.

There was a total of 125 personal authors; this included those 116 who were the authors of works which were cited eight or more times, plus the nine authors who were cited 15 or more times, but had no single work cited as many as eight times. Of these 125 authors, 89 (71.2%) were men, and 36 (28.8%) were women. In this group of 36 women, only 4 were not Americans. American women have been very active in librarianship since the 1880's. The first active female from this group of 32 Americans was Theresa Hitchler, who was placed in charge of a branch of the New York Free Circulating Library in 1888. Later, many women became active in the field, especially after Dewey's first class graduated in 1888. The other four non-Americans were three Britons, Dorothy May Norris, Lorna V. Paulin and Mary Piggott; and one Yugoslav, Eva Verona. These four have only been professionally active since approximately 1940. *If* this be indicative of the role of women in the field of librarianship, *then* it may be said that the *beginning* of "women's liberation" in *librarianship* had more than a fifty year head start in America than in other countries.

THE WORKS

The 184 most cited works were grouped according to the type of publication: monograph, periodical article, and *contribution* to a monograph or a paper presented at a conference. Of these three types, the most predominant was the monograph; there were 82 (44%) works classed as monographs, 73 (40%) were periodical articles, and 29 (16%) were contributions.

Of the 125 works published in the United States, the 80 periodical articles and contributions accounted for 64%, the 45 monographs make up only 36%. On the other hand, in Britain, the two periodical articles and the 11 contributions account for 45% of the 29 works, and the 16 monographs form 55%. The 30 works published in countries other than the United States and Great Britain are almost all monographs! Only 9 works (30%) were articles and contributions, while 21 (70%) were monographs.

One might react to the heavy use of periodical articles in the United States by saying that this was due to the fact that the United States was the first country to publish serials devoted to the field of cataloging and classification. But, this was proven *not* to be the case when the periodicals in which the

63 American articles appeared were examined. Of the 63 articles, 22 (35%) were published in *Library quarterly* and 13 (20%) in *Library journal*. Only 14 articles (22%) came out in *Catalogers' and classifiers' yearbook* and *Journal of cataloging and classification*. In essence, this means that 49 (78%) of the most cited articles in cataloging did *not* appear in serials specializing in this field.

THE PUBLISHERS

Because the majority of the 184 works were written by Americans it is not surprising that the big publishers are also American, but it is surprising that only three publishers produced almost one-half of the 184 works. The American Library Association published 41 (22.25%) of the works; the imprint of the University of Chicago appeared on 33 (17.9%) works; and the Government Printing Office in Washington issued 14 (7.6%). Thus these three were responsible for 88 (47.75%) of the 184 most cited works in cataloging. Apparently the Bradford distribution applies here as well.

PUBLICATION DATES

The dates of the 184 works range from 1841 to 1964, thus the network did include works from all eras. However, there are periods in this 125 year span which produced many more works than others. The two most prolific eras in the history of cataloging, as represented by these 184 works, are the decades of the 1930's and the 1950's. In the 1930's, 37 (20%) of the works appeared, and during the 1950's, 50 (27%) were published. In fact, 119 (64.66%) of the 184 works were written after 1930.

INTERRELATIONSHIPS AMONG THE AUTHORS

An endeavor was made to discover whether individuals writing on the same subject had personal contacts with others sharing the same interests. Data concerning the professional and personal lives of the 125 personal authors were searched in order to document a suspected continuous chain of personal contacts among all of the authors from Panizzi to those of today. Contacts forming such a chain among 115 of the most frequently cited authors were documented, or in cases where documentation was not possible, situations and circumstances were indicated in which there existed both the possibility and probability for personal contact. Many of the personal contacts were made in libraries and library schools, and at professional meetings and conferences. International relationships began when Jewett went to England in 1845 to visit Panizzi, and since then librarians from both America and Europe have been crossing the Atlantic to visit libraries and to confer with other librarians.

During the nineteenth century, it was possible to fully document personal contacts between individuals, but after the turn of the century it became necessary to point out relationships through institutions. This was due to the rapid and great increase in the number of libraries and librarians. Ten institutions were listed along with groups of persons whose periods of affiliation with each institution overlapped, thus forming a continuous vertical chain of contacts between a group of individuals at each institution. The groups of individuals at the ten institutions were connected through one or more persons who at one time or another were also associated with another institution. In this way a continuous horizontal linkage between the ten institutions was formed.

A continuous network of situations was created indicating that possibilities existed for at least 115 of the authors to have had personal contact with at least one other person from the whole group. There is no way to measure how *much* personal contact existed between these individuals. The degree of influence and the quality of ideas that may have passed from one mind to another await analysis in the field of intellectual history. But enough personal contacts and possibilities for contacts were documented to leave little doubt that what has been demonstrated was just a tiny tip of a huge iceberg.

INVISIBLE COLLEGES

After pointing out that interrelationships did indeed exist among 115 of the 125 most cited authors it became evident that there were ten individuals who could be considered "key figures" in various "invisible colleges." The various invisible colleges are not isolated and unrelated, but rather they are all linked by one or more individuals who belonged to one or more of these invisible colleges. Thus there is a time series or a chain of interlocking "invisible colleges" from the middle of the nineteenth century until this very day.

Without introducing any other relationships (that indubitably did exist among many of the 115 authors), an analysis of the data presented in Chapters V, VI, and VIII indicated that 90 (78.3%) of the 115 authors were connected through the ten "key figures." These ten are: Melvil Dewey, Louis Stanley Jast, James C. M. Hanson, William W. Bishop, Louis R. Wilson, Seymour Lubetzky, Herman H. Henkle, Andrew D. Osborn, Wyllis E. Wright, and Mary Piggott.

Each of these ten persons had contacts (or possible and probable contacts) with at least 12 of the other *most cited* authors. For this reason they deserve to be considered as "focal points" around which "invisible colleges" developed and functioned.

Table 15 lists the 90 authors and indicates with which of the key figures each had contacts as documented in Chapters V, VI, and VIII.

Table 16 shows the ten "key figures" and the groups of persons with whom each had contacts. In most cases, they were employed at the same institution simultaneously, or were speakers or other prominent persons at the same conference. In order to give the ten groups somewhat of a chronological order, they are arranged according to the birthdate of the "key figure," beginning with Dewey and ending with Piggott.

TABLE 15

List of Authors and the Key Figures With Whom Each Had Contacts

	Author	Key Figures
1.	Akers, Susan G.	Hanson, Wilson
2.	Allez, George C.	Hanson
3.	Angell, Richard S.	Hanson, Henkle, Lubetzky, Osborn, Piggott, Wright
4.	Arnold, Denis V.	Piggott
5.	Berthold, Arthur B.	Osborn, Wright
6.	Bishop, William W.	Hanson, Osborn
7.	Bostwick, Arthur E.	Hanson
8.	Branscomb, Harvie	Bishop
9.	Brown, James Duff	Dewey, Jast
10.	Burch, Vella Jane	Wilson
11.	Butcher, Stanley J.	Piggott
12.	Chaplin, Arthur H.	Lubetzky, Osborn, Piggott, Wright
13.	Childs, James B.	Henkle, Lubetzky
14.	Colvin, Laura C.	Bishop, Wright
15.	Coney, Donald	Bishop, Hanson, Wilson
16.	Currier, T. Franklin	Hanson
17.	Custer, Benjamin	Henkle, Lubetzky, Osborn, Wright
18.	Cutter, Charles A.	Dewey, Jast
19.	Dean, Hazel	Osborn, Wright
20.	Delisle, Leopold	Dewey, Jast
21.	Dewey, Melvil	Jast
22.	Dunkin, Paul S.	Henkle, Lubetzky, Osborn, Piggott, Wright
23.	Dziatzko, Karl	Dewey, Jast
24.	Ellinger, Werner B.	Henkle, Lubetzky, Osborn, Piggott, Wright
25.	Ellsworth, Ralph E.	Hanson, Wilson
26.	Fellows, Dorcas	Dewey
27.	Fletcher, William	Dewey, Hanson
28.	Francis, Frank C.	Lubetzky, Osborn, Piggott, Wright
29.	Gjelsness, Rudolph	Bishop, Hanson, Osborn, Wright
30.	Goodrich, Nathaniel	Dewey
31.	Gull, Cloyd Dake	Bishop, Henkle, Lubetzky, Osborn, Piggott, Wright
32.	Hand, Elinor	Henkle
33.	Hanson, James C. M.	Bishop, Osborn, Wilson
34.	Haskins, Susan M.	Bishop, Osborn
35.	Haygood, William C.	Hanson, Wilson
36.	Henkle, Herman H.	Lubetzky, Osborn

TABLE 15 (cont'd)

	Author	Key Figures
37.	Hiss, Sophie K.	Dewey
38.	Howe, Harriet E.	Hanson
39.	Jackson, Sidney L.	Osborn, Wright
40.	Jast, L. Stanley	Dewey
41.	Jolley, Leonard	Piggott
42.	Josephson, Aksel	Dewey
43.	Kingery, Robert E.	Osborn, Wright
44.	Lane, William C.	Dewey, Hanson, Jast
45.	Linderfelt, Klas A.	Dewey
46.	Lubetzky, Seymour	Henkle, Osborn, Piggott, Wright
47.	MacDonald, M. Ruth	Hanson
48.	MacNair, Mary W.	Bishop, Dewey, Hanson, Henkle
49.	MacPherson, Harriet	Hanson, Osborn, Wright
50.	Mann, Margaret	Bishop, Osborn
51.	Martel, Charles	Bishop, Hanson, Henkle, Lubetzky
52.	Mash, Maurice	Jast
53.	Metcalf, Keyes D.	Hanson, Osborn, Wright
54.	Miller, Robert A.	Hanson, Osborn, Wilson, Wright
55.	Mishoff, Willard O.	Bishop, Wilson
56.	Morsch, Lucile M.	Henkle, Lubetzky, Osborn, Wright
57.	Mortimer, Russell S.	Piggott
58.	Mudge, Isadore G.	Dewey, Hanson, Osborn
59.	Nyholm, Amy Wood	Henkle
60.	Osborn, Andrew D.	Bishop, Hanson, Lubetzky, Piggott, Wright
61.	Paulin, Lorna V.	Piggott
62.	Perkins, Frederic	Dewey
63.	Phillips, Philip Lee	Bishop, Hanson
64.	Pierson, Harriet W.	Bishop, Dewey, Hanson, Henkle
65.	Piggott, Mary	Lubetzky, Osborn, Wright
66.	Quinn, John Henry	Dewey, Jast
67.	Randall, William M.	Bishop, Hanson, Wilson
68.	Ranganathan, S. R.	Lubetzky, Osborn, Piggott, Wright
69.	Reichmann, Felix	Henkle, Lubetzky, Wilson
70.	Rider, Fremont	Dewey
71.	Savage, Ernest A.	Jast
72.	Sayers, W. C. Berwick	Jast
73.	Sharp, Henry Alexander	Jast
74.	Spalding, C. Sumner	Henkle, Lubetzky, Osborn, Piggott, Wright
75.	Stewart, James D.	Jast
76.	Strout, Ruth French	Henkle, Lubetzky, Osborn
77.	Swank, Raynard Coe	Lubetzky, Osborn, Wilson

TABLE 15 (cont'd)

	Author	Key Figures
78.	Taube, Mortimer	Hanson, Henkle
79.	Tauber, Maurice F.	Hanson, Osborn, Wilson, Wright
80.	Thom, Ian W.	Osborn, Wright
81.	Trotier, Arnold H.	Henkle
82.	Van Hoesen, Henry B.	Hanson, Wilson
83.	Ver Nooy, Winifred	Hanson, Henkle, Wilson
84.	Verona, Eva	Lubetzky, Osborn, Piggott, Wright
85.	Wallace, Ruth	Hanson
86.	Wells, Arthur J.	Piggott
87.	Wheatley, Henry B.	Dewey
88.	Whittemore, Caroline	Osborn, Wright
89.	Wilson, Louis R.	Hanson
90.	Wright, Wyllis Eaton	Lubetzky, Osborn, Piggott

TABLE 16
The Invisible Colleges

Group 1
"MELVIL DEWEY"

1. Brown, James Duff
2. Cutter, Charles Ammi
3. Delisle, Leopold
4. Dziatzko, Karl
5. Fellows, Dorcas
6. Fletcher, William I.
7. Goodrich, Nathaniel
8. Hiss, Sophie K.
9. Jast, L. Stanley
10. Josephson, Aksel
11. Lane, William C.
12. Linderfelt, Klas A.
13. MacNair, Mary W.
14. Mudge, Isadore G.
15. Perkins, Frederic
16. Pierson, Harriet W.
17. Quinn, John Henry
18. Rider, Fremont
19. Wheatley, Henry B.

Group 2
"L. STANLEY JAST"

1. Brown, James Duff
2. Cutter, Charles Ammi
3. Delisle, Leopold
4. Dewey, Melvil
5. Dziatzko, Karl
6. Lane, William C.
7. Mash, Maurice
8. Quinn, John Henry
9. Savage, Ernest A.
10. Sayers, W. C. Berwick
11. Sharp, Henry A.
12. Stewart, James D.

Group 3
"JAMES C. M. HANSON"

1. Akers, Susan G.
2. Allez, George C.
3. Angell, Richard S.

TABLE 16 (cont'd)

Group 3 (cont'd)

4. Bishop, William W.
5. Bostwick, Arthur E.
6. Coney, Donald
7. Currier, T. Franklin
8. Ellsworth, Ralph E.
9. Fletcher, William I.
10. Gjelsness, Rudolph H.
11. Haygood, William C.
12. Howe, Harriet Emma
13. Lane, William C.
14. MacDonald, M. Ruth
15. MacNair, Mary W.
16. MacPherson, Harriet D.
17. Martel, Charles
18. Metcalf, Keyes D.
19. Miller, Robert A.
20. Mudge, Isadore G.
21. Osborn, Andrew D.
22. Phillips, Philip Lee
23. Pierson, Harriet W.
24. Randall, William M.
25. Taube, Mortimer
26. Tauber, Maurice F.
27. Van Hoesen, Henry B.
28. Ver Nooy, Winifred
29. Wallace, Ruth
30. Wilson, Louis R.

Group 4
"WILLIAM W. BISHOP"

1. Branscomb, Harvie
2. Colvin, Laura C.
3. Coney, Donald
4. Gjelsness, Rudolph H.
5. Gull, Cloyd Dake
6. Hanson, James C. M.
7. Haskins, Susan M.
8. MacNair, Mary W.
9. Mann, Margaret
10. Martel, Charles
11. Mishoff, Willard O.
12. Osborn, Andrew D.

Group 4 (cont'd)

13. Phillips, Philip Lee
14. Pierson, Harriet W.
15. Randall, William M.

Group 5
"LOUIS R. WILSON"

1. Akers, Susan G.
2. Burch, Vella Jane
3. Coney, Donald
4. Ellsworth, Ralph E.
5. Hanson, James C. M.
6. Haygood, William C.
7. Miller, Robert A.
8. Mishoff, Willard O.
9. Randall, William M.
10. Reichmann, Felix
11. Swank, Raynard C.
12. Tauber, Maurice F.
13. Van Hoesen, Henry B.
14. Ver Nooy, Winifred

Group 6
"SEYMOUR LUBETZKY"

1. Angell, Richard S.
2. Chaplin, Arthur H.
3. Childs, James B.
4. Custer, Benjamin
5. Dunkin, Paul S.
6. Ellinger, Werner B.
7. Francis, Frank C.
8. Gull, Cloyd Dake
9. Henkle, Herman H.
10. Martel, Charles
11. Morsch, Lucile M.
12. Osborn, Andrew D.
13. Piggott, Mary
14. Ranganathan, S. R.
15. Reichmann, Felix
16. Spalding, C. Sumner
17. Strout, Ruth F.
18. Swank, Raynard C.

TABLE 16 (cont'd)

Group 6 (cont'd)

19. Verona, Eva
20. Wright, Wyllis E.

Group 7
"HERMAN H. HENKLE"

1. Angell, Richard S.
2. Childs, James B.
3. Custer, Benjamin
4. Dunkin, Paul S.
5. Ellinger, Werner B.
6. Gull, Cloyd Dake
7. Hand, Elinor
8. Lubetzky, Seymour
9. MacNair, Mary W.
10. Martel, Charles
11. Morsch, Lucile M.
12. Nyholm, Amy Wood
13. Pierson, Harriet W.
14. Reichmann, Felix
15. Spalding, C. Sumner
16. Strout, Ruth F.
17. Taube, Mortimer
18. Trotier, Arnold H.
19. Ver Nooy, Winifred

Group 8
"ANDREW D. OSBORN"

1. Angell, Richard S.
2. Berthold, Arthur B.
3. Bishop, William W.
4. Chaplin, Arthur H.
5. Custer, Benjamin
6. Dean, Hazel
7. Dunkin, Paul S.
8. Ellinger, Werner B.
9. Francis, Frank C.
10. Gjelsness, Ruldolph H.
11. Gull, Cloyd Dake
12. Hanson, James C. M.
13. Haskins, Susan M.
14. Henkle, Herman H.

Group 8 (cont'd)

15. Jackson, Sidney L.
16. Kingery, Robert E.
17. Lubetzky, Seymour
18. MacPherson, Harriet D.
19. Mann, Margaret
20. Metcalf, Keyes D.
21. Miller, Robert A.
22. Morsch, Lucile M.
23. Mudge, Isadore G.
24. Piggott, Mary
25. Ranganathan, S. R.
26. Spalding, C. Sumner
27. Strout, Ruth F.
28. Swank, Raynard C.
29. Tauber, Maurice F.
30. Thom, Ian W.
31. Verona, Eva
32. Whittemore, Caroline
33. Wright, Wyllis E.

Group 9
"WYLLIS E. WRIGHT"

1. Angell, Richard S.
2. Berthold, Arthur B.
3. Chaplin, Arthur H.
4. Colvin, Laura C.
5. Custer, Benjamin
6. Dean, Hazel
7. Dunkin, Paul S.
8. Ellinger, Werner B.
9. Francis, Frank C.
10. Gjelsness, Rudolph H.
11. Gull, Cloyd Dake
12. Jackson, Sidney L.
13. Kingery, Robert E.
14. Lubetzky, Seymour
15. MacPherson, Harriet D.
16. Metcalf, Keyes D.
17. Miller, Robert A.
18. Morsch, Lucile M.
19. Osborn, Andrew D.
20. Piggott, Mary

TABLE 16 (cont'd)

Group 9 (cont'd)

21. Ranganathan, S. R.
22. Spalding, C. Sumner
23. Tauber, Maurice F.
24. Thom, Ian W.
25. Verona, Eva
26. Whittemore, Caroline

Group 10
"MARY PIGGOTT"

1. Angell, Richard S.
2. Arnold, Denis V.
3. Butcher, Stanley J.
4. Chaplin, Arthur H.

Group 10 (cont'd)

5. Dunkin, Paul S.
6. Ellinger, Werner B.
7. Francis, Frank G.
8. Gull, Cloyd Dake
9. Jolley, Leonard
10. Lubetzky, Seymour
11. Mortimer, Russell S.
12. Osborn, Andrew D.
13. Paulin, Lorna V.
14. Ranganathan, S. R.
15. Spalding, C. Sumner
16. Verona, Eva
17. Wells, Arthur J.
18. Wright, Wyllis E.

Melvil Dewey can be considered the "father of modern librarianship"; he was the principal activist for the library movement that began in America in 1876. He also founded the *first* library school and many of his students became quite prominent in the field.

In Britain, Louis Stanley Jast was associated with many British catalogers of distinction, all of whom were at one time or another connected with the Croydon Public Libraries. Surprisingly, after Panizzi, it was the Croydon Public Libraries and *not* the British Museum that became the institution in which so much cataloging history was made.

During the first four decades of the twentieth century, James C. M. Hanson, William W. Bishop and Louis R. Wilson were central figures in America. Hanson was at the Library of Congress for 14 years, and from there went to the University of Chicago in 1910. Almost 20 years later he became the first professor of the new Graduate Library School at the University of Chicago, and for most of his stay there he also lectured at Columbia University's School of Library Service. William W. Bishop, after spending five years as a librarian at Princeton University, went to the Library of Congress in 1907 as superintendent of the reading room. In 1915 he became the librarian at the University of Michigan, and later in 1926 he was the first director of its new library school. He remained at the University of Michigan until his retirement in 1941. Louis R. Wilson was chosen as director of the University of Chicago's Graduate Library School from 1932 to 1942, when he returned to the University of North Carolina as professor in the library school there.

Since 1940 the key figures are Seymour Lubetzky, Herman Henkle, Andrew Osborn, Wyllis Wright and Mary Piggott. Seymour Lubetzky and Herman Henkle were at the Library of Congress in the 1940's. Lubetzky

remained there until 1960. During his last two decades at the Library of Congress, Lubetzky was a catalyst in the movement for catalog code revision. He did most of the intellectual work involved in making a logical code.
Henkle left the Library of Congress in 1947 and three years afterwards became the director of the John Crerar Library in Chicago. Also, during the years of his directorship at the John Crerar Library he was a lecturer at the Graduate Library School of the University of Chicago.

Andrew D. Osborn and Wyllis E. Wright were both at the New York Public Library in the late 1920's and the 1930's. In 1938, Osborn went to Harvard University where he remained for the next 20 years. Wyllis Wright became the chief cataloger at New York Public Library in 1936 and held this post until 1945. During most of this time, he was also associated with the library school at Columbia University.

Mary Piggott was at the County Branch Library, Ormskirk, Lancashire (England) during the 1940's, and served as a lecturer at the University of London School of Librarianship during the 1950's and 1960's.

Lubetzky, Osborn, Wright and Piggott were all very prominent and active figures in the development of the new Anglo-American cataloging code during the 1950's and the 1960's.

Thus, in essence, there have been ten key persons in a series of "invisible colleges" around whom the development and growth of cataloging centered. This focus was not only due to their intellectual contributions, but also because of their vast number of personal contacts, professional interrelationships, and the impact of their reputations.

SIGNIFICANT INSTITUTIONS

A careful study of the ten institutions and the most cited librarians who were associated with them indicated that 56 of the authors in this study at one time or another had been affiliated with just five of those institutions. These five were: Columbia University, University of Chicago, Library of Congress, New York Public Library, and the University of Michigan.

An analysis of the periods in which these 56 authors were present at the five institutions suggested that there were eras in which each place had many of these frequently cited authors, while at other times almost no one from this group was present.

If one considers these 56 librarians as important in the field of cataloging, and *if* their presence at an institution is interpreted as a measure of importance to that institution's tribute to cataloging, *then* the following statements are justified.

During the first quarter of the twentieth century the Library of Congress was *the* important library in cataloging. In the late 1920's and during the 1930's the University of Chicago and Columbia University were the two institutions excelling in the subject. Also during this same period the University of Michigan and the New York Public Library reached their zenith (at least in cataloging), but this was nowhere near the level reached by Columbia and Chicago.

During the 1920's few catalogers went to the Library of Congress. No new person went to the "national library" during the 1930's. However, after 1940 many of the most cited authors seemed to flock to the Library of Congress, and since then it has been the leading library in the field of cataloging.

KUDOS

The election to prominent positions and honors awarded are indications of important contributions to a profession. The "Margaret Mann Citation in Cataloging and Classification" was established in 1950, and since its first awarding in 1951, no less than 13 of the most cited authors in this study have been recipients. No doubt it was an even greater honor to another author in this group when this award was named for Margaret Mann in recognition of her many contributions to cataloging. Catalogers are also important to the profession as a whole. Ten of the frequently cited authors were elected President of the American Library Association, and six to the presidency of the Library Association of the United Kingdom. One author was prominent in both areas: Lucile M. Morsch (Mrs. Werner B. Ellinger) was awarded the first Margaret Mann Citation in 1951, and also was President of the American Library Association in the 1957-1958 term.

It cannot be denied that such honors bestowed on members of a profession are indeed a measure of their significant contributions. Of the 125 personal authors in this study, 29 (23.2%) have been honored either by their election as President of a national library association or through the Margaret Mann Citation in Cataloging and Classification.

THE MOST FREQUENTLY CITED WORKS

The total number of times that a work was cited could not be used to judge its value, whether cited a thousand times or never cited. In this study only cited works could emerge, and even at that, the number of citations alone could not be a determining factor in assessing worth or importance. However, "citation frequency," when coupled with "citation duration" has proved to be a better way to measure the worth or "impact" of a writing. This must not be construed as the *best*, but only as an improvement, however slight this might be.

Many studies have revealed that very few, that is, probably less than one percent, of all writings are ever cited 20 or more years after their publication. All works in this study which were cited at least 15 times were sorted out and an analysis of the "citation duration" was made. The purpose of this analysis was to determine the length of time during which these works were referred to by other writers. The 58 works which had been cited 15 or more times were classified into nine groups. This classification was based on the citation duration, the aspect of cataloging treated, and the type of prediction or general statements that could be made about a specified group of works.

SUPERCLASSICS, CLASSICS AND POTENTIAL CLASSICS

The first group contained works which had a citation duration of more than 75 years, and were called "superclassics." Six works fell into this group, three American and three British; all published between 1841 and 1889. It was pointed out that Charles A. Cutter must have made quite an impact on the profession, because he was the author of *two* superclassics.

There were eight works which had a citation duration of 50 years or more and these were called "classics." Six of these were "cataloging codes" and were published in a 25 year period, 1883-1908. The other two "classics" were Graesel's *Handbuch* and Quinn's *Library cataloguing*.

The six superclassics and the eight classics were works which continued to be cited for long periods of time after their original publication date. Writings which were cited so often and for more than 50 years, must have indeed made an impact on the profession.

The remaining writings with long citation durations, "potential classics," are grouped by type. There were six cataloging codes published in the second quarter of the twentieth century. The citation duration of these six works ranged from 20 to 39 years, and the citation frequency from 22 to 65, which suggests that they may be considered as potential classics.

Two works dealing with corporate entry published in 1935 were still being cited in 1964. These, too, may be considered as potential classics. A citation duration of three decades is indicative of some impact.

Among cataloging manuals, six of the eight manuals included in this group were among the 14 most cited works of the entire study. Their citation frequency ranged from 35 to 81 and the citation duration from 33 to 47 years. The superimposition of citation duration graphs showed that after the publication of the manuals of Susan Akers and Margaret Mann, that Theresa Hitchler's manual was cited much less and eventually fell into disuse, that is, was no longer cited. Again, it was pointed out that the high citation frequency of these manuals in conjunction with the long citation duration indicated their impact in the field of cataloging.

Of several writings on library catalogs, one of these, Cutter's *Library catalogues*, was considered a superclassic and has been discussed earlier. Fletcher's "Future of the catalog" was cited 21 times and had a citation duration of 49 years. Undoubtedly, it will prove to be a classic.

Among the six works dealing with theory and history, there were two German publications, both of which had a citation duration of more than 40 years and each had a citation frequency of 17. The other four works in this category were American and their citation duration was shorter, from 25 to 32 years, but their citation frequency was greater, from 20 to 45.

The above mentioned 43 works all have long citation durations and those not already considered as superclassics or classics are all definitely potentials. However, it must be pointed out that there were 50 works published before 1950 that were cited 15 or more times; of these 50, 48 had a citation duration of no less than 20 years. Judgment must be deferred until the future.

Finally, there were two other groups of works, those which were considered moribund, due to the fact that they had not been cited recently and their graphs indicated they were slowly declining in use, and those which were published between 1950 and 1960 were declared to be too new to be able to judge their potential.

Part 2—Discussion

CITATION DURATION

The coupling of "citation duration" with "citation frequency" brought out some aspects that citation frequency alone could never have done. Panizzi's *Rules...* and Cutter's *Library catalogues* were only cited 15 times each, but the citation duration was 79 and 78 years, respectively, hence they qualified as "superclassics" according to the criteria established herein. Another superclassic, Cutter's *Rules for a dictionary catalog*, was the most cited work with a citation frequency of 138, and it had a citation duration of 85 years. Lubetzky was the most cited author of the entire study, yet not a single work by him qualified as a "classic" because the *time factor* did not permit such recent publications to be termed classics. The high citation frequency of Lubetzky's works most certainly indicated that they were potential classics. A similar case was Margaret Mann's introductory text which had a high citation frequency, but its publication date was too recent to give it a citation duration of no more than 33 years. All in all, citation frequency joined with citation duration gave a much better vantage point from which to evaluate a work's impact on the field.

THE NETWORK VERSUS A BODY OF LITERATURE

One question arises concerning the possible difference between the results of a study in which citations were taken from the entire body of literature on cataloging and those results obtained from a network emanating from the citations of a single work. This brings up some interesting questions. If the whole body of literature were used, would Cutter's *Rules for a dictionary catalog* be the most cited work? Would Lubetzky be the most cited personal author? Would the proportion of monographs and journal articles be the same? Would the decades of the 1930's and the 1950's be the predominant publication dates? Would Americans constitute 62% of the authors, and be responsible for 67% of all the publications? Would the same 184 works be the most cited? Would their rank order according to citation frequency (Table 13) remain the same? Would the citation duration patterns discussed in Chapter IX be greatly changed or remain basically the same? These and other questions remain to be answered by future investigators. Their answers will help judge the method employed in this study.

QUANTITATIVE COLLECTIVE BIOGRAPHY
(PROSOPOGRAPHY)

The procedure used here for identifying a core literature also identified a group of 125 frequently cited authors. The 125 personal authors were used as a universe and several questions were asked concerning the life of each in order to determine whom else he contacted in the membership of this universe. The professional careers of these 125 authors covered the entire span of this study, that is, from 1835 to 1969. The basic questions asked were: (1) when and where did he study? (2) with which libraries, library schools and other institutions was the person associated throughout his career? (3) to which professional organizations did he belong? (4) which conferences and meetings did he attend, and on which committees or councils did he serve? (5) what other personal contacts did he have with any of the others in this group?

This use of prosopography, or multiple career-line analysis, showed that personal contacts among 115 of the authors either could be proven, or at least it was possible to document situations in which it was definitely possible and highly probable that personal contact did occur. For example, the fact that *two catalogers* were employed at the same library simultaneously would indicate the high probability that they did communicate with each other. They probably even worked in the same room.

An analysis of the totality of these contacts uncovered a chain of "invisible colleges" over time, encompassing librarians from Panizzi to Lubetzky. Contacts among 90 of these individuals were established, and, in fact, ten individuals were considered "key figures" because the entire chain of invisible colleges could be constructed around these persons. Several of the 90 individuals had contact *with at least six* of the ten key figures. Thus, the algorithm used for identifying a core literature also identified a chain of "invisible colleges" and served to point out the probable existence of an almost infinite number of interrelationships among the authors of this core literature.

IMPLICATIONS FOR FURTHER RESEARCH

This study raises other questions about other subject literatures. Will the algorithm used here identify core literatures in other areas? Is the outcome of any such study affected by the fact that some subject literatures appear basically in monographs, while others appear principally in journal articles? Do the hard sciences, arts and humanities, the social sciences, and other areas differ so greatly one from the others that this algorithm could not be used universally for *all* subject literatures?

Many other inquiries are needed to find out the answers to these and many other questions, and it is hoped that this investigation will inspire further research and serve as a foundation for others who may be induced to undertake such studies.

APPENDIX I

THE MOST FREQUENTLY CITED WORKS

The following list contains full bibliographic detail of all the editions and versions of the 184 works that were most often cited in the network. The number in parentheses at the right of each author indicates the number of times that the work appeared in the network.

1. Adams, Winona Josephine (11)
    "A divided catalog in practice," *PNLA quarterly*, 7:48-50, October 1942.
2. Akers, Susan Grey (37)
    Simple library cataloging. 4th ed. Chicago, A.L.A., 1954. 250p.
    Akers, Susan Grey
    Simple library cataloging. 3d ed. rewritten. Chicago, A.L.A., 1944. 197p.
    Akers, Susan Grey
    Simple library cataloging. 2d ed. rewritten. Chicago, A.L.A., 1933. 173p.
    Akers, Susan Grey
    Simple library cataloging. Chicago, A.L.A., 1927. 95p.
3. Akers, Susan Grey (8)
    "The relation of the professional and clerical division of cataloging activities to cataloging courses," *Library quarterly*, 5:101-136, January 1935.
4. Akers, Susan Grey (12)
    "To what extent do the students of the liberal-arts colleges use the bibliographic items given on the catalogue card?," *Library quarterly*, 1:394-408, October 1931.
5. Allez, George Clare (17)
    "In defence of the alphabetical subject catalog," *Wilson bulletin*, 13: 242-243, December 1938.
6. Alvord, Dorothy Maria (8)
    "King County Public Library does it with IBM," *PNLA quarterly*, 16: 123-132, April 1952.
7. American Library Association (26)
    A.L.A. catalog rules; author and title entries. Preliminary American second edition. Chicago, 1941. 408p.
8. American Library Association (65)
    A.L.A. cataloging rules for author and title entries. 2d ed. Chicago, 1949. 265p.

9. American Library Association and the (British) Library Association (96)
    Catalog rules; author and title entries. Chicago, 1908. 88p.
10. American Library Association (16)
    Condensed rules for an author and title catalog. Washington, Govt. Print. Off., 1904. 28p.
    American Library Association
    Condensed rules for an author and title catalog. Washington, Govt. Print. Off., 1902. 23p.
    American Library Association
    "Condensed rules for an author and title catalog," *Library journal,* 8:251-254, September-October, 1883.
11. American Library Association (15)
    A survey of the libraries in the United States. v.4, Chicago, 1927. 267p.
12. Angell, Richard Sloane (9)
    "The need for a new United States code," *Library quarterly,* 26: 318-330, October 1956.
13. Arnold, Denis Victor (11)
    "Punched card systems for cataloguing and indexing." In: Piggott, Mary. *Cataloguing principles and practice; an inquiry.* London, The Library Association, 1954. pp. 88-92.
14. Baldwin, Emma V. and William E. Marcus (9)
    Library costs and budgets; a study of cost accounting in public libraries. New York, Bowker, 1941. 201p.
15. Bauhuis, Walter (10)
    "Katalogreformen," *Zeitschrift für Bibliothekswesen und Bibliographie,* 1:185-208, 1954.
16. Berthold, Arthur Benedict (8)
    "Form sub-headings under government bodies." In: Institute on Cataloging Code Revision, Stanford University, 1958. *Working papers.* Stanford, Calif., 1958. Paper no. 6, 3p.
17. Berthold, Arthur Benedict (9)
    "The future of the catalog in research libraries," *College and research libraries,* 8:20-22, and 53, January 1947.
18. Bishop, William Warner (40)
    Practical handbook of modern library cataloging. 2d ed. Baltimore, Williams & Wilkins, 1924. 152p.
    Bishop, William Warner
    Practical handbook of modern library cataloging. Baltimore, Williams & Wilkins, 1914. 150p.
19. Bishop, William Warner (14)
    "Some considerations on the cost of cataloging," *Library journal,* 30:10-14, January 1905.
20. Bodleian Library (8)
    Rules for the author-catalogue of books published in or after 1920. Oxford, The University Press, 1923. 55p.

21. Boggs, Samuel W. and Dorothy C. Lewis (12)
    The classification and cataloging of maps and atlases. New York, Special Libraries Association, 1945. 175p.
    Boggs, Samuel W. and Dorothy C. Lewis
    The classification and cataloging of maps and atlases. [Preliminary edition.] Washington, 1932. 159 leaves.
22. Bostwick, Arthur Elmore (11)
    The American public library. 4th ed. rev. and enlarged. New York, Appleton, 1929. 471p.
    Bostwick, Arthur Elmore
    The American public library. 3d ed. New York, Appleton, 1917. 414p.
    Bostwick, Arthur Elmore
    The American public library. [2d ed.] New York, Appleton, 1917. 396p.
    Bostwick, Arthur Elmore
    The American public library. New York, Appleton, 1910. 393p.
23. Branscomb, Bennett Harvie (10)
    Teaching with books; a study of college libraries. Chicago, A.L.A., 1940. 239p.
24. British Museum (16)
    "Report of the Commissioners appointed to inquire into the constitution and government of the British Museum, with minutes of evidence." In: Great Britain. Parliament. House of Commons. *Reports from Commissioners.* v.5. London, 1850. 823p.
25. British Museum (29)
    Rules for compiling the catalogues of printed books, maps and music in the British Museum. Rev. ed. London, 1936. 67p.
    British Museum
    Rules for compiling the catalogues of printed books, maps and music in the British Museum. London, 1927. 64p.
    British Museum
    Rules for compiling the catalogues of printed books, maps and music in the British Museum. London, 1920. 62p.
    British Museum
    Rules for compiling the catalogues of printed books, maps and music in the British Museum. London, 1906. 44p.
    British Museum
    Rules for compiling the catalogues of printed books, maps and music in the British Museum. London, 1900. 40p.
26. Brown, James Duff (13)
    Library classification and cataloguing. London, Libraco, 1912. 261p.
27. Brown, James Duff (17)
    Manual of library economy. 5th ed. by W. C. Berwick Sayers. London, Grafton, 1937. 591p.
    Brown, James Duff
    Manual of library economy. 4th ed. London, Grafton, 1931. 533p.

Brown, James Duff
Manual of library economy. 3d ed. New York, Wilson, 1920. 519p.
Brown, James Duff
Manual of library economy. Rev. ed. London, London Supply Co., 1907. 422p.
Brown, James Duff
Manual of library economy. London, Scott, Greenwood, 1903. 476p.

28. Buelow, Bertha Elizabeth (8)
"Cataloging costs," *Library journal*, 60:657-659, September 2, 1935.
29. Burch, Vella Jane (11)
"The divided catalog; Duke University Library faces the future," *College and research libraries*, 3:219-223, June 1942.
30. Butcher, Stanley Jack (11)
"Cataloguing in municipal libraries." In: Piggott, Mary. *Cataloguing principles and practice; an inquiry.* London, The Library Association, 1954. pp. 93-103.
31. Cambridge University. Library. (13)
Rules for the catalogues of printed books, maps and music. Cambridge, The University Press, 1927. 77 leaves.
32. Chaplin, Arthur Hugh (19)
"A reconsideration of the British Museum rules for compiling the catalogues of printed books—II." In: Piggott, Mary. *Cataloguing principles and practice; an inquiry.* London, The Library Association, 1954. pp. 37-49.
33. Chaplin, Arthur Hugh (10)
"A universal cataloging code," *Library quarterly*, 26:337-347, October 1956.
34. Childs, James Bennett (16)
Author entry for government publications. Washington, Govt. Print. Off., 1939. 38p.
Childs, James Bennett
"Author entry for government publications." In: *Public documents; their selection, distribution, cataloging, reproduction and preservation. Papers presented at the 1934 conference of the American Library Association.* Chicago, A.L.A., 1935. pp. 103-128.
35. Colvin, Laura Catherine (9)
"Entry of all institutions under name rather than place." In: Institute on Cataloging Code Revision, Stanford University, 1958. *Working papers.* Stanford, Calif., 1958. Paper no. 5, 35p.
36. Coney, Donald (9)
"The administration of technical processes." In: Joeckel, Carleton B. *Current issues in library administration.* Chicago, University of Chicago Press, 1939. pp. 163-180.
37. Currier, Thomas Franklin (8)
"Selective cataloging at the Harvard Library," *Library journal*, 46: 673-677, August 1924.

38. Custer, Benjamin Allen (9)
    "Some unanswered questions: the public library," *Library quarterly*, 26:356-361, October 1956.
39. Cutter, Charles Ammi (11)
    "Corporate entry; further considerations," *Library journal*, 22:432-434, September 1897.
40. Cutter, Charles Ammi (15)
    "Library catalogues." In: U.S. Bureau of Education. *Public libraries in the United States of America; their history, condition, and management.* Washington, Govt. Print. Off., 1876. pp. 526-622.
41. Cutter, Charles Ammi (138)
    Rules for a dictionary catalog. 4th ed., rewritten. Washington, Govt. Print. Off., 1904. 173p.

    Cutter, Charles Ammi
    Rules for a dictionary catalog. 3d ed. Washington, Govt. Print. Off., 1891. 140p.

    Cutter, Charles Ammi
    Rules for a dictionary catalog. 2d ed. Washington, Govt. Print. Off., 1889. 133p.

    Cutter, Charles Ammi
    "Rules for a printed dictionary catalogue." In: U.S. Bureau of Education. *Public libraries in the United States of America; their history, condition, and management.* Part 2. Washington, Govt. Print. Off., 1876. 89p.
42. Dean, Hazel (9)
    "Comments on the Lubetzky report by a cataloging teacher," *Journal of cataloging and classification*, 9:135-137, September 1953.
43. Dean, Hazel (17)
    "Shall we divide our catalog vertically?," *Catalogers' and classifiers' yearbook*, no. 8, 1939. Chicago, A.L.A., 1940. pp. 43-47.
44. Delisle, Leopold Victor (14)
    Instructions elementaires et techniques pour la mise et le maintien en ordre des livres d'une bibliotheque. 4 ed. Paris, Champion, 1910. 94p.

    Delisle, Leopold Victor
    Instructions elementaires et techniques pour la mise et le maintien en ordre des livres d'une bibliotheque. Paris, Champion, 1908. 82p.

    Delisle, Leopold Victor
    Instructions elementaires et techniques pour la mise et le maintien en ordre des livres d'une bibliotheque. Lille, Danel, 1890. 76p.
45. Denmark, Bogsamlingskomite (10)
    Katalogisering; raad og regler til brug ved ordingen af bogsamlinger udgivet af Statens Bogsamlingskomite. København, 1917. 48p.
46. Dewey, Melvil (16)
    Library school rules. 5th ed. Boston, Library Bureau, 1905. 72p.

    Dewey, Melvil
    Library school rules. 4th ed. Boston, Library Bureau, 1899. 72p.

Dewey, Melvil
Library school rules. 3d ed. Boston, Library Bureau, 1894. 72p.
Dewey, Melvil
Library school rules. 2d ed. Boston, Library Bureau, 1892. 75p.
47. Dewey, Melvil (11)
Simplified library school rules. Boston, Library Bureau, 1912. 96p.
Dewey, Melvil
Simplified library school rules. Boston, Library Bureau, 1904. 96p.
Dewey, Melvil
Simplified library school rules. Boston, Library Bureau, 1898. 96p.
48. Dunkin, Paul Shaner (15)
"Criticisms of current cataloging practice," *Library quarterly*, 26: 286-302, October 1956.
49. Dziatzko, Karl (13)
Instruction für die Ordnung der Titel im alphabetischen Zettelkatalog der Königlichen und Universitäts-Bibliothek zu Breslau. Berlin, Asher, 1886. 74p.
Dziatzko, Karl
Regole per il catalogo alfabetico a schede della Reale biblioteca universitaria di Breslavia. Firenze, Sansoni, 1887. 110p.
50. Edwards, Edward (12)
Memoirs of libraries, including a handbook of library economy. London, Trübner, 1859, 2v.
51. Ellinger, Werner Bruno (8)
"Form sub-headings." In: Institute on Cataloging Code Revision, Stanford University, 1958. *Summary of proceedings*. Stanford, Calif., 1958. pp. 53-57.
52. Ellsworth, Ralph Eugene (8)
"The administrative implications for university libraries of the new cataloging code," *College and research libraries*, 3:134-138, March 1942.
53. Ellsworth, Ralph Eugene (10)
"Notes on the Lubetzky report," *Journal of cataloging and classification*, 9:130-131, September 1953.
54. Esdaile, Arundell James Kennedy (8)
A student's manual of bibliography. 3d ed. London, Allen & Unwin, 1954. 392p.
Esdaile, Arundell James Kennedy
A student's manual of bibliography. London, Allen & Unwin, 1931. 383p.
55. Fellows, Jennie Dorcas (43)
Cataloging rules, with explanations and illustrations. 2d ed., rev. and enl. New York, Wilson, 1926. 303p.
Fellows, Jennie Dorcas
Cataloging rules prepared for the course in elementary cataloging, New York State Library School. Preliminary ed. Albany, The University of the State of New York, 1914. 181p.

56. Field, Frances Bernice (8)
"Serial entry." In: Institute on Cataloging Code Revision, Stanford University, 1958. *Working papers*. Stanford, Calif., 1958. Paper no. 3, 26p.
57. Fletcher, William Isaac (10)
"Corporate authorship," *Library journal*, 21:493-494, November 1896.
58. Fletcher, William Isaac (21)
"The future of the catalog," *Library journal*, 30:141-144, March 1905.
59. Francis, Frank Chalton (13)
"A reconsideration of the British Museum rules for compiling the catalogues of printed books—I." In: Piggott, Mary. *Cataloguing principles and practice; an inquiry*. London, The Library Association, 1954. pp. 26-36.
60. Frels, Wilhelm (17)
Die bibliothekarische Titelaufnahme in Deutschland. Leipzig, Harrassowitz, 1919. 54p. (Beihefte zum Zentralblatt für Bibliothekswesen, nr. 47.)
61. Fuchs, Hermann (9)
"Für und wider die *Preussischen Instruktionen*," *Zeitschrift für Bibliothekswesen und Bibliographie*, 1:173-185, 1954.
62. Fumagalli, Giuseppe (12)
Cataloghi di biblioteche e indici bibliografici. Firenze, Sansoni, 1887. 199p.
63. Gifford, Florence Marguerite (10)
"A reference librarian's point of view applied to the Lubetzky critique," *Journal of cataloging and classification*, 9:132-134, September 1953.
64. Graesel, Arnim (20)
Handbuch der bibliothekslehre. 2 voelig umgearb. aufl. der "Grundzüge der bibliothekslehre, neuarbeitung von dr. Jul. Petzholdts Katechismus der bibliothekslehre." Leipzig, Weber, 1902. 563p.

Graesel, Arnim
Grundzüge der bibliothekslehre mit bibliographischen und erläuternden anmerkungen. Leipzig, Weber, 1890. 424p.

Graesel, Arnim
Manuel de bibliotheconomie. Traduction de Jules Laude. Paris, Welter, 1897. 628p.

Graesel, Arnim
Manual del bibliotecario. Santiago de Chile, 1914.
65. Gull, Cloyd Dake (8)
"Substitutes for the card catalog," *Library trends*, 2:318-329, October 1953.
66. Hagedorn, Ralph K. (12)
"Toward catalog reform," *Library journal*, 64:223-225, March 15, 1939.

67. Hand, Elinor (10)
"A cost survey in a university library," *Library journal*, 55:763-766, October 1, 1930.
68. Hanson, James C. M. (22)
A comparative study of cataloging rules based on the Anglo-American code of 1908. Chicago, University of Chicago Press, 1939. 144p.
69. Hanson, James C. M. (20)
"Corporate authorship versus title entry," *Library quarterly*, 5:457-466, October 1935.
70. Hanson, James C. M. (10)
"Rules for corporate entry," *Library journal*, 30:72-80, February 1905.
71. Hanson, James C. M. (12)
"Sound and unsound economy in cataloguing," *Library quarterly*, 4:65-75, January 1934.
72. Haskins, Susan McCallum (8)
"Problems of subdivisions in the entries for corporate bodies." In: Institute on Cataloging Code Revision, Stanford University, 1958. *Working papers*. Stanford, Calif., 1958. Paper no. 8, 19p.
73. Haskins, Susan McCallum (9)
"Something new in cataloging," *College and research libraries*, 6: 291-296 and 321, September 1945.
74. Haskins, Susan McCallum (13)
"Stepping stone to a new catalog code," *Journal of cataloging and classification*, 9:125-130, September 1953.
75. Haygood, William Converse (8)
Who uses the public library; a survey of the patrons of the Circulation and Reference Departments of the New York Public Library. Chicago, University of Chicago Press, 1938. 137p.
76. Henkle, Herman Henry (12)
Studies of descriptive cataloging; a report to the Librarian of Congress by the Director of the Processing Department. Washington, Govt. Print. Off., 1946. 48p.
77. Herrick, Mary Darrah (8)
"Entry for works of single authorship and anonyma." In: Institute on Cataloging Code Revision, Stanford University, 1958. *Working papers*. Stanford, Calif., 1958. Paper no. 2, 11p.
78. Hesse, Leopold Auguste Constantin (9)
Bibliotheconomie; ou Nouveau manuel complet pour l'arrangement, la conservation et l'administration des bibliotheques, par L. A. Constantin. Nouvelle ed. Paris, Roret, 1841. 266p.
79. Hiss, Sophie Knowlton (9)
"Economies in cataloging," *Catalogers' and classifiers' yearbook*, no. 4, 1934. Chicago, A.L.A., 1935. pp. 39-49.
80. Hitchler, Theresa (35)
Cataloging for small libraries. 3d enl. ed. New York, Stechert, 1926. 316p.

Hitchler, Theresa
Cataloging for small libraries. Rev. ed. Chicago, A.L.A., 1915. 316p.
Hitchler, Theresa
Cataloging for small libraries. Boston, A.L.A., 1905. 84p.
81. Howe, Harriet Emma (8)
The catalog. Revised. Chicago, A.L.A., 1927. 24p.
82. Institute on Cataloging Code Revision, Stanford University, 1958. (8)
Summary of proceedings. Stanford, Calif., 1958. 62p.
83. International Federation of Library Associations. Working Group on the Coordination of Cataloging Principles (10)
"Report on anonyma and works of corporate authorship," *Libri*, 6: 271-297, 1956.
84. Italy. Direzione generale delle accademie e biblioteche (20)
Regole per la compilazione del catalogo alfabetico per autori nelle biblioteche italiane. Roma, Fratelli Palombi, 1956. 133p.
Italy. Direzione generale delle accademie e biblioteche
Regole per la compilazione del catalogo alfabetico per autori nelle biblioteche italiane. Roma, Istituto poligrafico dello Stato, 1932. 95p.
Italy. Direzione generale delle accademie e biblioteche
Regole per la compilazione del catalogo alfabetico per autori nelle biblioteche italiane. Roma, Nardecchia, 1922.
85. Jackson, Sidney Louis (9)
Catalog use study. Chicago, A.L.A., 1958. 86p.
86. Jewett, Charles Coffin (38)
On the construction of catalogues of libraries and their publication by means of separate, stereotyped titles. With rules and examples. 2d ed. Washington, Smithsonian Institution, 1853. 96p.
Jewett, Charles Coffin
On the construction of catalogues of libraries and their publication by means of separate, stereotyped titles. With rules and examples. Washington, Smithsonian Institution, 1852. 78p.
Jewett, Charles Coffin
Della compilazione dei cataloghi per biblioteche e del modo di publicarli per mezzo di titoli separati stereopati. Firenze, Sansoni, 1888. 120p.
87. Jewett, Charles Coffin (9)
"A plan for stereotyping catalogues by separate titles, and for forming a general stereotyped catalogue of public libraries in the United States." In: American Association for the Advancement of Science. *Proceedings* [of the] fourth meeting held at New Haven, Conn., August, 1850. Washington, 1851. pp. 165-176.
88. Johnson, Margaret F. and Dorothy E. Cook (10)
Manual of cataloging and classification for small school and public libraries. 4th ed. New York, Wilson, 1950. 71p.

Johnson, Margaret F. and Dorothy E. Cook
Manual of cataloging and classification for small school and public libraries. 3d ed. New York, Wilson, 1939. 78p.

Johnson, Margaret F.
Manual of cataloging and classification for elementary school librarians. New York, Wilson, 1929. 45p.

89. Jolley, Leonard Julier (11)
"Cataloguing in special libraries." In: Piggott, Mary. *Cataloguing principles and practice; an inquiry.* London, The Library Association, 1954. pp. 130-l44.

90. Jolley, Leonard Julier (9)
"Some recent developments in cataloguing in the U.S.A.," *Journal of documentation,* 6:70-82, June 1950.

91. Josephson, Aksel Gustav Salomon (9)
"The cataloging test; results and outlook," *Library journal,* 41:654-657, September 1916.

92. Kaiser, Rudolf (11)
"Die Katalogisierung." In: Milkau, Fritz. *Handbuch der Bibliothekswissenschaft.* v.2. Leipzig, Harrassowitz, 1933. pp. 237-318.

93. Kaiser, Rudolf (8)
"Neuere ausländische Instruktionen für alphabetische Kataloge," *Zentralblatt für Bibliothekswesen,* 35:101-119, Mai-Juni 1918.

94. Kaiser, Rudolf (17)
"Vergleichung der englisch-amerikanischen Katalogregeln mit der preussischen Instruktion und die Frage einer internationalen Einigung," *Zentralblatt für Bibliothekswesen,* 28:412-430, September-Oktober 1911.

95. Keysser, Adolf (8)
"Ueber die Einrichtung der alphabetischen Hauptkataloge öffentlicher Bibliotheken," *Zentralblatt für Bibliothekswesen,* 2:1-19, Januar 1885.

96. Kungliga Biblioteket, Stockholm (9)
Provisoriska katalogregler för Kungliga Biblioteket. Ny översedd upplaga. Stockholm, 1958. 33 leaves.

Kungliga Biblioteket, Stockholm
Katalogregler för Kungl. Biblioteket. Stockholm, 1916. 138p.

97. Ledos, Eugene Gabriel (9)
Usages suivis dans la redaction du Catalogue general des livres imprimes de la Bibliotheque nationale. Nouvelle ed. Paris, Bibliotheque nationale, 1940.

Ledos, Eugene Gabriel
Usages suivis dans la redaction du Catalogue general des livres imprimes de la Bibliotheque nationale. Paris, Champion, 1923. 70p.

98. Library of Congress (31)
Rules for descriptive cataloging in the Library of Congress. Washington, 1949. 141p.

99. Library of Congress (9)
    Rules for descriptive cataloging in the Library of Congress. Supplement, 1949-51. Washington, 1952. 19p.
100. Library of Congress (14)
    Rules for descriptive cataloging in the Library of Congress: motion pictures and filmstrips. 2d preliminary ed. Washington, 1953. 18p.
    Library of Congress
    Rules for descriptive cataloging in the Library of Congress: motion pictures and filmstrips. Preliminary ed. Washington, 1952. 12p.
101. Library of Congress (9)
    Rules for descriptive cataloging in the Library of Congress: phonorecords. 2d preliminary ed. Washington, 1964. 11p.
    Library of Congress
    Rules for descriptive cataloging in the Library of Congress: phonorecords. Preliminary ed. Washington, 1952. 10p.
102. Linderfelt, Klas August (23)
    Eclectic card catalog rules; author and title entries. Boston, Charles A. Cutter, 1890. 104p.
103. Lubetzky, Seymour (15)
    "The cataloging of publications of corporate authors; a rejoinder," *Library quarterly*, 21:1-12, January 1951.
104. Lubetzky, Seymour (54)
    Cataloging rules and principles; a critique of the A.L.A. rules for entry and a proposed design for their revision. Washington, Govt. Print. Off., 1953. 65p.
105. Lubetzky, Seymour (17)
    Code of cataloging rules; author and title entry. Chicago, A.L.A., 1960. 86p.
106. Lubetzky, Seymour (12)
    "Comments on discussion of cataloging rules and principles," *Journal of cataloging and classification*, 9:137-142, September 1953.
107. Lubetzky, Seymour (13)
    "Crisis in the catalog," *Catalogers' and classifiers' yearbook*, no. 8, 1939. Chicago, A.L.A., 1940. pp. 48-54.
108. Lubetzky, Seymour (8)
    "Development of cataloging rules," *Library trends*, 2:179-186, October 1953.
109. Lubetzky, Seymour (11)
    "Some observations on revision of the cataloging code," *Library quarterly*, 26: 362-366, October 1956.
110. MacNair, Mary Wilson (17)
    Guide to the cataloguing of periodicals. 3d ed. Washington, Govt. Print. Off., 1925. 23p.
    MacNair, Mary Wilson
    Guide to the cataloguing of periodicals. 2d ed. Washington, Govt. Print. Off., 1920. 23p.

MacNair, Mary Wilson
Guide to the cataloguing of periodicals. Washington, Govt. Print. Off., 1918. 23p.
111. MacPherson, Harriet Dorothea (26)
Some practical problems in cataloging. Chicago, A.L.A., 1936. 131p.
112. Maire, Albert (9)
Manuel pratique du bibliothecaire. Paris, A. Picard, 1896. 591p.
113. Mann, Margaret (81)
Introduction to cataloging and the classification of books. 2d ed. Chicago, A.L.A., 1943. 276p.

Mann, Margaret
Introduction to cataloging and the classification of books. Chicago, A.L.A., 1930. 424p.
114. Mann, Margaret (8)
"The teaching of technical processes." In: Randall, William M. *The acquisition and cataloging of books*. Chicago, University of Chicago Press, 1940. pp. 355-381.
115. Martel, Charles (8)
"Cataloging 1876-1926," *Library journal*, 51:1065-1069, December 1, 1926.
116. Mash, Maurice H. B. (8)
"Cataloguing codes," *The librarian and book world*, 4:135-140, 155-158, 195-199 and 239-241, November and December 1913, and January and February 1914.
117. Mecklenburg, Hermann Benno (9)
"Zu Dr. Keysser's Aufsatz über die alphabetischen Hauptkataloge," *Zentralblatt für Bibliothekswesen*, 2:91-96, März 1885.
118. Miller, Robert Alexander (9)
Cost accounting for libraries; a technique for determining the labor costs of acquisition and cataloging work. Unpublished Ph.D. dissertation, University of Chicago, 1936. 193p.
119. Miller, Robert Alexander (11)
"Cost accounting for libraries; acquisition and cataloging," *Library quarterly*, 7:511-536, October 1937.
120. Miller, Robert Alexander (9)
"Costs of technical operations." In: Randall, William M. *The acquisition and cataloging of books*. Chicago, University of Chicago Press, 1940. pp. 220-238.
121. Miller, Robert Alexander (8)
"On the use of the card catalog," *Library quarterly*, 12:629-637, July 1942.
122. Mishoff, Willard Oral (9)
"The catalog from a reader's viewpoint," *Library journal*, 57:1035-1038, December 15, 1932.
123. Mortimer, Russell Stanley (11)
"Cataloguing in university libraries." In: Piggott, Mary. *Cataloguing principles and practice; an inquiry*. London, The Library Association, 1954. pp. 111-129.

124. Mudge, Isadore Gilbert (24)
"Present day economies in cataloging," *Catalogers' and classifiers' yearbook*, no. 4, 1934. Chicago, A.L.A., 1935. pp. 9-49.
125. Music Library Association (9)
Code for cataloging music. Washington, 1941-42. 1 vol.
126. Norris, Dorothy May (11)
A history of cataloguing and cataloguing methods, 1100-1850. London, Grafton, 1939. 246p.
127. Norsk bibliotekforening (9)
Katalogiseringsregler for norske biblioteker. 3 rev. utg. Oslo, 1955. 112p.
Norsk bibliotekforening
Katalogiseringsregler for norske biblioteker. 2 rev. utg. Oslo, 1938. 92p.
Norsk bibliotekforening
Katalogiseringsregler for norske biblioteker. Oslo, 1925. 72p.
128. Nyholm, Amy Wood (15)
"California divides its catalog," *Library journal*, 63:723-726, October 1, 1938.
129. Nyholm, Amy Wood (13)
"California examines its divided catalogs," *College and research libraries*, 9:195-201, July 1948.
130. Nyholm, Amy Wood (13)
"The large dictionary catalog faces der Tag," *Catalogers' and classifiers' yearbook*, no. 8, 1939. Chicago, A.L.A., 1940. pp. 39-42.
131. Osborn, Andrew D. and Susan M. Haskins (10)
"Catalog maintenance," *Library trends*, 2:279-289, October 1953.
132. Osborn, Andrew D. (13)
"Cataloging and cataloging codes in other countries today," *Library quarterly*, 26:276-285, October 1956.
133. Osborn, Andrew D. (8)
"Cataloging costs and a changing conception of cataloging," *Catalogers' and classifiers' yearbook*, no. 5, 1936. Chicago, A.L.A., 1936. pp. 45-54.
134. Osborn, Andrew D. (9)
"Cataloging developments in the United States, 1940-1947." In: International Federation of Library Associations. *Actes du Comite International des Bibliotheques*. 13eme session, Oslo, 20-22 mai, 1947. La Haye, Martinus Nijhoff, 1947. pp. 68-72.
135. Osborn, Andrew D. (45)
"The crisis in cataloging," *Library quarterly*, 11:393-411, October 1941.
136. Panizzi, Sir Anthony (15)
"Rules for the compilation of the catalogue." In: British Museum. *Catalogue of printed books*, v.1. London, 1841. pp. v-ix.
137. Paulin, Lorna Vincent (11)
"Cataloguing in county libraries." In: Piggott, Mary. *Cataloguing principles and practice; an inquiry*. London, The Library Association, 1954. pp. 104-110.

138. Perkins, Frederic Beecher (8)
San Francisco cataloguing for public libraries; a manual of the system used in the San Francisco Public Library. San Francisco, C. A. Murdock, 1884. 53p.
139. Pettee, Julia (20)
"The development of authorship entry and the formulation of authorship rules as found in the Anglo-American code," *Library quarterly*, 6:270-290, July 1936.
140. Phillips, Philip Lee (9)
Notes on the cataloging, care and classification of maps and atlases. Rev. ed. Washington, Govt. Print. Off., 1921. 21p.
Phillips, Philip Lee
Notes on the cataloging, care and classification of maps and atlases. Washington, Govt. Print. Off., 1915. 20p.
141. Pierce, Watson O'Dell (9)
Work measurement in public libraries. New York, Social Science Research Council, 1949. 238p.
142. Pierson, Harriet Wheeler (24)
Guide to the cataloguing of the serial publications of societies and institutions. 2d ed. Washington, Govt. Print. Off., 1931. 128p.
Pierson, Harriet Wheeler
Guide to the cataloguing of the serial publications of societies and institutions. Washington, Govt. Print. Off., 1919. 108p.
143. Piggott, Mary (13)
"Introduction; a survey of the present situation." In her *Cataloguing principles and practice; an inquiry.* London, The Library Association, 1954. pp. 1-14.
144. Prussian instructions (38)
The Prussian instructions; rules for the alphabetical catalogs of the Prussian libraries. Translated from the second edition, authorized August 10, 1908. With an introduction and notes by Andrew D. Osborn. Ann Arbor, University of Michigan Press, 1938. 192p.
Prussian instructions
Instruktionen für die alphabetischen Kataloge der preussischen Bibliotheken. 2 ausg. vom 10 Mai 1899. Berlin, Behrend, 1915. 179p.
Prussian instructions
Instruktionen für die alphabetischen Kataloge der preussischen Bibliotheken. 2 ausg. Berlin, Behrend, 1909. 179p.
Prussian instructions
Instruktionen für die alphabetischen Kataloge der preussischen Bibliotheken. Berlin, Asher, 1899. 163p.
145. Quinn, John Henry (28)
Library cataloguing. London, Truslove & Hanson, 1913. 256p.
Quinn, John Henry
Manual of library cataloguing. London, Library Supply Co., 1899. 164p.

146. Quinn, John Henry and Henry Waldo Acomb (13)
A manual of cataloguing and indexing. Rev. 2d ed. London, Allen & Unwin, 1937. 286p.
Quinn, John Henry and Henry Waldo Acomb
A manual of cataloguing and indexing. London, Allen & Unwin, 1933. 286p.
147. Randall, William Madison (12)
"The technical processes and library service." In his *The acquisition and cataloging of books.* Chicago, University of Chicago Press, 1940. pp. 1-29.
148. Randall, William Madison (8)
"The uses of library catalogs; a research project," *Catalogers' and classifiers' yearbook,* no. 2, 1930. Chicago, A.L.A., 1931. pp. 24-32.
149. Ranganathan, Shiyali Ramamrita (22)
Classified catalogue code. 4th ed. Madras, Madras Library Association, 1958. 605p.
Ranganathan, Shiyali Ramamrita
Classified catalogue code. 3d ed. Madras, Madras Library Association, 1952. 401p.
Ranganathan, Shiyali Ramamrita
Classified catalogue code. 2d ed. Madras, Madras Library Association, 1945. 328p.
Ranganathan, Shiyali Ramamrita
Classified catalogue code. Madras, Madras Library Association, 1934. 292p.
150. Ranganathan, Shiyali Ramamrita (11)
The five laws of library science. 2d ed. Madras, Madras Library Association, 1957. 456p.
Ranganathan, Shiyali Ramamrita
The five laws of library science. Madras, Madras Library Association, 1931. 458p.
151. Ranganathan, Shiyali Ramamrita (20)
Heading and canons; comparative study of five catalogue codes. Madras, Viswanathan, 1955. 300p.
152. Ranganathan, Shiyali Ramamrita (15)
Theory of library catalogue. Madras, Madras Library Association, 1938. 393p.
153. Reichmann, Felix (13)
"Costs of cataloging," *Library trends,* 2:290-317, October 1953.
154. Rider, Arthur Fremont (19)
"Alternatives for the present dictionary catalog." In: Randall, William M. *The acquisition and cataloging of books.* Chicago, University of Chicago Press, 1940. pp. 133-162.
155. Rider, Arthur Fremont (15)
"Library cost accounting," *Library quarterly,* 6:331-381, October 1936.

156. Rider, Arthur Fremont (19)
"The possibility of discarding the card catalog," *Library quarterly*, 8:329-345, July 1938.
157. Rouveyre, Edouard (8)
Les connaissances necessaires a un bibliophile. v.2. 5eme ed. Paris, E. Rouveyre, 1899.
158. Savage, Ernest Albert (8)
Manual of descriptive annotation for library catalogues. London, Library Supply Co., 1906. 155p.
159. Sayers, W. C. Berwick and James Stewart (14)
The card catalogue; a practical manual for public and private libraries. London, Grafton, 1913. 86p.
160. Schneider, Georg (8)
Theory and history of bibliography. New York, Columbia University Press, 1934. 306p.
Schneider, Georg
Handbuch der Bibliographie. 2 aufl. Leipzig, Hiersemann, 1924. 544p.
Schneider, Georg
Handbuch der Bibliographie. Leipzig, Hiersemann, 1923. 544p.
Schneider, Georg
Einführung in die Bibliographie. Leipzig, Hiersemann, 1936. 203p.
161. Sharp, Henry Alexander (37)
Cataloguing; a textbook for use in libraries. 4th ed. London, Grafton, 1948. 388p.
Sharp, Henry Alexander
Cataloguing; a textbook for use in libraries. 3d ed. London, Grafton, 1944. 406p.
Sharp, Henry Alexander
Cataloguing; a textbook for use in libraries. 2d ed. London, Grafton, 1937. 472p.
Sharp, Henry Alexander
Cataloguing; a textbook for use in libraries. London, Grafton, 1935. 314p.
162. Sharp, Henry Alexander (12)
"Current research in cataloguing." In: Piggott, Mary. *Cataloguing principles and practice; an inquiry.* London, The Library Association, 1954. pp. 15-25.
163. Spain. Junta Técnica de Archivos, Bibliotecas y Museos (10)
Instrucciones para la redacción del catálogo alfabético de autores y obras anónimas en las bibliotecas públicas del Estado. 3a ed. reformada. Madrid, 1964. 264p.
Spain. Junta Técnica de Archivos, Bibliotecas y Museos
Instrucciones para la redacción del catálogo alfabético de autores y obras anónimas en las bibliotecas públicas del Estado. 2a ed. Madrid, 1941. 184p.

Spain. Junta Facultativa de Archivos, Bibliotecas y Museos
Instrucciones para la redacción del catálogo alfabético de autores y obras anónimas en las bibliotecas públicas del Estado. Edición oficial. Madrid, 1926. 198p.

Spain. Junta Facultativa de Archivos, Bibliotecas y Museos
Instrucciones para la redacción del catálogo alfabético de autores y obras anónimas en las bibliotecas públicas del Estado. Madrid, 1912. 166p.

Spain. Junta Facultativa de Archivos, Bibliotecas y Museos
Instrucciones para la redacción del catálogo alfabético de autores y obras anónimas en las bibliotecas públicas del Estado. Madrid, 1902. 152p.

164. Stewart, James Douglas (13)
The sheaf catalogue; a practical handbook on the compilation of manuscript catalogues for public and private libraries. London, Libraco, 1909. 55p.

165. Strout, Ruth French (10)
"The development of the catalog and cataloging codes," *Library quarterly*, 26: 254-275, October 1956.

166. Swank, Raynard Coe (9)
"Cataloging cost factors," *Library quarterly*, 26:303-317, October 1956.

167. Swank, Raynard Coe (15)
"The cataloging department in the library organization," *Library quarterly*, 18:24-32, January 1948.

168. Taube, Mortimer (26)
"The cataloging of publications of corporate authors," *Library quarterly*, 20:1-20, January 1950.

169. Tauber, Maurice Falcolm (13)
"Reclassification and recataloging of materials in college and university libraries." In: Randall, William M. *The acquisition and cataloging of books*. Chicago, University of Chicago Press, 1940. pp. 187-219.

170. Tauber, Maurice Falcolm (15)
Technical services in libraries. New York, Columbia University Press, 1954. 487p.

171. Thom, Ian Walter (10)
"The divided catalog in college and university libraries," *College and research libraries*, 10:236-241, July 1949.

172. Van Hoesen, Henry Bartlett (13)
Selective cataloging. New York, Wilson, 1928. 131p.

173. Vatican Library (47)
Rules for the catalog of printed books. Translated from the second Italian edition. Edited by Wyllis E. Wright. Chicago, A.L.A., 1948. 426p.

Vatican Library
Norme per il catalogo degli stampati. 3 ed. Citta del Vaticano, Biblioteca apostólica vaticana, 1949. 396p.

Vatican Library
Norme per il catalogo degli stampati. 2 ed. Citta del Vaticano, Biblioteca apostólica vaticana, 1939. 490p.

Vatican Library
Norme per il catalogo degli stampati. Citta del Vaticano, Biblioteca apostólica vaticana, 1931. 400p.

Vatican Library
Normas para catalogación de impresos. Edición española. Ciudad del Vaticano, Biblioteca Apostólica Vaticana, 1940. 472p.

Vatican Library
Normas para catalogaçao de impresos. Ed. brasileira. Sao Paulo, Instituto Progresso, 1949. 341p.

174. Ver Nooy, Winifred (18)
"The consumer and the catalog." In: Randall, William M. *The acquisition and cataloging of books*. Chicago, University of Chicago Press, 1940. pp. 310-330.

175. Verona, Eva (13)
"Literary unit versus bibliographical unit," *Libri*, 9:79-104, 1959.

176. Wallace, Ruth (10)
The care and treatment of music in a library. Chicago, A.L.A., 1927. 76p.

177. Watkins, David Roy (8)
"A reference librarian looks at the proposed catalog code." In: Institute on Catalog Code Revision, McGill University, 1960. *Working papers*. Chicago, 1960. Paper no. 9, 6p.

178. Wells, Arthur James (13)
"New developments in cataloguing in the *British National Bibliography*." In: Piggott, Mary. *Cataloguing principles and practice; an inquiry*. London, The Library Association, 1954. pp. 50-63.

179. Wheatley, Henry Benjamin (22)
How to catalogue a library. 2d ed. London, Elliot Stock, 1889. 268p.

180. Whittemore, Caroline and Nathaniel L. Goodrich (10)
"Crisis in the cards," *Dartmouth College library bulletin*, 3:151-154, December 1941.

181. Wilson, Louis R. and Maurice F. Tauber (9)
The university library; its organization, administration, and functions. 2d ed. Chicago, University of Chicago Press, 1956. 641p.

Wilson, Louis R. and Maurice F. Tauber
The university library; its organization, administration, and functions. Chicago, University of Chicago Press, 1945. 570p.

182. Wright, Wyllis Eaton (16)
"Horizontal division of the catalog," *Catalogers' and classifiers' yearbook*, no. 8, 1939. Chicago, A.L.A., 1940. pp. 55-57.

183. Wright, Wyllis Eaton (11)
    "A report of progress on catalog code revision in the United States," *Library quarterly*, 26:331-336, October 1956.
184. Wright, Wyllis Eaton (8)
    "Some fundamental principles in cataloging," *Catalogers' and classifiers' yearbook*, no. 7, 1938. Chicago, A.L.A., 1938. pp. 26-39.

APPENDIX II

THE MOST OFTEN CITED AUTHORS

PART A—AUTHORS OF WORKS WHICH WERE CITED EIGHT OR MORE TIMES

1. Acomb, Henry Waldo, 1891-
2. Adams, Winona Josephine, 1903-
3. Akers, Susan Grey, 1889-
4. Allez, George Clare, 1897-1950
5. Alvord, Dorothy Maria, 1895-
6. American Library Association
7. Angell, Richard Sloane, 1905-
8. Arnold, Denis Victor, 1915-
9. Baldwin, Emma Virginia, 1877-1952
10. Bauhuis, Walter, 1905-1961
11. Berthold, Arthur Benedict, 1905-
12. Bishop, William Warner, 1871-1955
13. Bodleian Library
14. Boggs, Samuel Whittemore, 1889-1954
15. Bostwick, Arthur Elmore, 1860-1942
16. Branscomb, Bennett Harvie, 1894-
17. British Museum
18. Brown, James Duff, 1862-1914
19. Buelow, Bertha Elizabeth, 1904-
20. Burch, Vella Jane, 1910-
21. Butcher, Stanley Jack, fl. 1946-
22. Cambridge University. Library.

    Carnovsky, Ruth French *see* Strout, Ruth French

23. Chaplin, Arthur Hugh, 1905-
24. Childs, James Bennett, 1896-
25. Colvin, Laura Catherine, 1905-
26. Coney, Donald, 1901-1973
27. Currier, Thomas Franklin, 1873-1946
28. Custer, Benjamin Allen, 1912-
29. Cutter, Charles Ammi, 1837-1903
30. Dean, Hazel, 1893-
31. Delisle, Leopold Victor, 1826-1910
32. Denmark. Bogsamlingskomite
33. Dewey, Melvil, 1851-1931
34. Dunkin, Paul Shaner, 1905-
35. Dziatzko, Karl, 1842-1903
36. Edwards, Edward, 1812-1886
37. Ellinger, Werner Bruno, 1908-1972
38. Ellsworth, Ralph Eugene, 1907-
39. Esdaile, Arundell James Kennedy, 1880-1956
40. Fellows, Jennie Dorcas, 1873-1938
41. Field, Frances Bernice, 1906-
42. Fletcher, William Isaac, 1844-1917
43. Francis, Frank Chalton, 1901-
44. Frels, Wilhelm, 1886-1942
45. Fuchs, Hermann, 1896-
46. Fumagalli, Giuseppe, 1863-1939
47. Gifford, Florence Marguerite, 1890-
48. Goodrich, Nathaniel Lewis, 1880-1957
49. Graesel, Arnim, 1849-1917
50. Gull, Cloyd Dake, 1915-
51. Hagedorn, Ralph Karl, 1912-

52. Hand, Elinor, fl. 1930-
53. Hanson, James Christian Meinich, 1864-1943
54. Haskins, Susan McCallum, 1907-
55. Haygood, William Converse, 1910-
56. Henkle, Herman Henry, 1900-
57. Herrick, Mary Darrah, 1908-
58. Hesse, Leopold Auguste Constantin, 1779-1884

Hickox, Elinor Hand *see* Hand, Elinor

59. Hiss, Sophie Knowlton, 1881-
60. Hitchler, Theresa, 1867-1955
61. Howe, Harriet Emma, 1881-1965
62. Institute on Catalog Code Revision
63. International Federation of Library Associations
64. Italy. Direzione generale delle accademie e biblioteche
65. Jackson, Sidney Louis, 1914-
66. Jewett, Charles Coffin, 1816-1868
67. Johnson, Margaret Fullerton, 1894-
68. Jolley, Leonard Julier, 1914-
69. Josephson, Aksel Gustav Salomon, 1860-1944
70. Kaiser, Rudolf, 1862-1937
71. Keysser, Adolf, 1850-1932
72. Kungliga Biblioteket, Stockholm
73. Ledos, Eugene Gabriel, 1864-
74. Lewis, Dorothy Cornwell, 1899-
75. The Library Association
76. Library of Congress
77. Linderfelt, Klas August, 1847-1900
78. Lubetzky, Seymour, 1898-
79. MacNair, Mary Wilson, 1873-1972
80. MacPherson, Harriet Dorothea, 1892-1967
81. Maire, Albert, 1856-
82. Mann, Margaret, 1873-1960
83. Marcus, William Elder, 1883-
84. Martel, Charles, 1860-1945
85. Mash, Maurice Harry Brett, d. 1942
86. Mecklenburg, Hermann Benno, 1848-1887
87. Miller, Robert Alexander, 1907-
88. Mishoff, Willard Oral, 1896-
89. Mortimer, Russell Stanley, 1914-
90. Mudge, Isadore Gilbert, 1875-1957
91. Music Library Association
92. Norris, Dorothy May, 1909-
93. Norsk bibliotekforening
94. Nyholm, Amy Fredericka Wood, 1907-
95. Osborn, Andrew Delbridge, 1902-
96. Panizzi, Sir Anthony, 1797-1879
97. Paulin, Lorna Vincent, 1914-
98. Perkins, Frederic Beecher, 1828-1899
99. Pettee, Julia, 1872-1967
100. Phillips, Philip Lee, 1857-1924
101. Pierce, Watson O'Dell, 1904-
102. Pierson, Harriet Wheeler, 1874-1966
103. Piggott, Mary, fl. 1942-
104. Prussian instructions
105. Quinn, John Henry, 1860-1941
106. Randall, William Madison, 1899-
107. Ranganathan, Shiyali Ramamrita, 1892-1972
108. Reichmann, Felix, 1899-
109. Rider, Arthur Fremont, 1885-1962
110. Rouveyre, Edouard, 1849-
111. Savage, Ernest Albert, 1877-1966
112. Sayers, William Charles Berwick, 1881-1960
113. Schneider, Georg, 1876-

114. Sharp, Henry Alexander, 1886-1962
115. Spain. Junta Técnica de Archivos, Bibliotecas y Museos
116. Stewart, James Douglas, 1880-1965
117. Strout, Ruth French, 1908-
118. Swank, Raynard Coe, 1912-
119. Taube, Mortimer, 1910-1965
120. Tauber, Maurice Falcolm, 1908-
121. Thom, Ian Walter, 1911-
122. Van Hoesen, Henry Bartlett, 1885-1965
123. Vatican Library
124. Ver Nooy, Winifred, 1891-
125. Verona, Eva, fl. 1941-
126. Wallace, Ruth, 1879-
127. Watkins, David Roy, 1915-
128. Wells, Arthur James, 1912-
129. Wheatley, Henry Benjamin, 1838-1917
130. Whittemore, Caroline, 1897-
131. Wilson, Louis Round, 1876-

Wood, Amy Fredericka *see* Nyholm, Amy Fredericka Wood

132. Wright, Wyllis Eaton, 1903-

PART B—FREQUENTLY CITED AUTHORS WHICH HAD NO SINGLE WORK CITED AS MANY AS EIGHT TIMES

Ellinger, Lucile M. *see* Morsch, Lucile M.

1. Gjelsness, Rudolph H., 1894-1969
2. Jast, Louis Stanley, 1868-1944
3. Kingery, Robert Ernest, 1913-
4. Lane, William Coolidge, 1859-1931
5. MacDonald, Margaret Ruth, 1904-
6. Metcalf, Keyes DeWitt, 1899-
7. Morsch, Lucile M., 1906-1972
8. Spalding, Charles Sumner, 1912-
9. Trotier, Arnold Herman, 1899-

APPENDIX III

USES AND ANALYSES OF CITATION PATTERNS: A SELECT BIBLIOGRAPHY

An important criterion for inclusion in this bibliography was the examination of each item by the author. The arrangement is in chronological order to point out the historical development and trends in the use and analysis of citation patterns.

1927
    Gross, P. L. K. and E. M. Gross
        "College libraries and chemical education." *Science*, 66:385-389, October 28, 1927.
    Hart, Hornell
        "The history of social thought: a consensus of American opinion." *Social forces*, 6:190-196, December 1927.

1929
    Allen, Edward S.
        "Periodicals for mathematicians." *Science*, 70:592-594, December 20, 1929.

1930
    McNeely, J. K. and C. D. Crosno
        "Periodicals for electrical engineers." *Science*, 72:81-84, July 25, 1930.

1931
    Gross, P. L. K. and A. C. Woodford
        "Serial literature used by American geologists." *Science*, 73:660-664, June 19, 1931.
    Jenkins, R. L.
        "Periodicals for medical libraries." *Journal of the American Medical Association*, 97:608-610, August 30, 1931.

1932
    Jenkins, R. L.
        "Periodicals for child-guidance clinics." *Mental hygiene*, 16:624-630, October 1932.
    Sherwood, K. K.
        "Relative value of medical magazines." *Northwest medicine*, 31:273-276, June 1932.

1934

Louttit, C. M. and Lillian L. Lockridge
"Psychological journals." *American journal of psychology*, 46:147-148, January 1934.

Mengert, William F.
"Periodicals on endocrinology of sex." *Endocrinology*, 18:421-422, May-June 1934.

1935

Gregory, Jennie
"An evaluation of periodical literature from the standpoint of endocrinology." *Endocrinology*, 19:213-215, March-April 1935.

Hooker, Ruth H.
"A study of scientific periodicals." *Review of scientific instruments*, 6:333-338, November 1935.

Sheppard, Oden E.
"The chemistry student still needs a reading knowledge of German." *Journal of chemical education*, 12:472-473, October 1935.

1936

Hackh, Ingo
"The periodicals useful in the dental library." *Bulletin of the Medical Library Association*, 25:109-112, September 1936.

1937

Dalziel, Charles F.
"Evaluation of periodicals for electrical engineers." *Library quarterly*, 7:354-372, July 1937.

Gregory, Jennie
"An evaluation of medical periodicals." *Bulletin of the Medical Library Association*, 25:172-188, February 1937.

1938

Barnard, Cyril C.
"The selection of periodicals for medical and scientific libraries." *Library Association record*, 5:549-557, November 1938.

Dalziel, Charles F.
"Journals for electrical engineers." *Electrical engineering*, 57:110-113, March 1938.

Henkle, Herman H.
"The periodical literature of biochemistry." *Bulletin of the Medical Library Association*, 27:139-147, December 1938.

1940

Patterson, Austin M.
"Journal citations in the 'Recueil', 1937-1939." *Recueil des travaux chimiques des Pays-Bas*, 59:538-544, 1940.

1941

Croft, Kenneth
"Periodical publications and agricultural analysis; a bibliographical study." *Journal of chemical education*, 18:315-316, July 1941.

1942

Casey, Albert E.
"Influence of individual North American and British journals on medical progress in the United States and Britain." *Bulletin of the Medical Library Association*, 30:464-466, October 1942.

1944

Brodman, Estelle
"Choosing physiology journals." *Bulletin of the Medical Library Association*, 32:479-483, October 1944.

Smith, Maurice H.
"The selection of chemical engineering periodicals in college libraries." *College and research libraries*, 5:217-227, June 1944.

1945

Banay, George L.
"The use of research publications in mental disease." *Bulletin of the Medical Library Association*, 33:50-59, January 1945.

Patterson, Austin M.
"Literature references in 'Industrial and Engineering Chemistry' for 1939." *Journal of chemical education*, 22:514-515, October 1945.

1946

Postell, William Dosite
"Further comments on the mathematical analysis of evaluating scientific journals." *Bulletin of the Medical Library Association*, 34:107-109, April 1946.

1947

Voigt, Melvin J.
"Scientific periodicals as a basic requirement for engineering and agricultural research." *College and research libraries*, 7:354-359 and 375, July 1947.

1949

Fussler, Herman H.
"Characteristics of the research literature used by chemists and physicists in the United States: Part I." *Library quarterly*, 19:19-35, January 1949.

Fussler, Herman H.
"Characteristics of the research literature used by chemists and physicists in the United States: Part II." *Library quarterly*, 19:119-143, April 1949.

1951

Tolpin, J. G., et al.
"The scientific literature cited by Russian organic chemists." *Journal of chemical education*, 28:254-258, May 1951.

1952

Broadus, Robert N.
"An analysis of literature cited in the American Sociological Review." *American sociological review*, 17:355-357, June 1952.

1953

Broadus, Robert N.
"The literature of educational research." *School and society*, 77:8-10, January 3, 1953.
Broadus, Robert N.
The research literature of the field of speech. Chicago, Association of College and Reference Libraries, 1953. pp. 22-31. (ACRL monographs, no. 7.)
Stevens, Rolland Elwell
Characteristics of subject literatures. Chicago, Association of College and Reference Libraries, 1953. pp. 10-21. (ACRL monographs, no. 6.)

1955

Adair, W. C.
"Citation indexes for scientific literature?" *American documentation*, 6:31-32, January 1955.
Friis, Th.
"The use of citation analysis as a research technique and its implications for libraries." *South African libraries*, 23:12-15, July 1955.
Garfield, Eugene
"Citation indexes for science." *Science*, 122:108-111, July 15, 1955.

1956

Brown, Charles Harvey
Scientific serials; characteristics and lists of most cited publications in mathematics, physics, chemistry, geology, physiology, botany, zoology, and entomology. Chicago, Association of College and Reference Libraries, 1956. (ACRL monographs, no. 16.) 189p.

1957

Barrett, Richard L. and Mildred A. Barrett
"Journals most cited by chemists and chemical engineers." *Journal of chemical education*, 34:35-38, January 1957.
Louttit, C. M.
"The use of foreign languages by psychologists, chemists, and physicists." *American journal of psychology*, 70:314-316, June 1957.

Morgan, Melvin B.
"Characteristics of the periodical literature of physiology used in the United States and Canada." *American journal of physiology*, 191: 416-421, November 1957.

1959

Burton, Robert E.
"Citations in American engineering journals: I. Chemical engineering." *American documentation*, 10:70-73, January 1959.

Burton, Robert E.
"Citations in American engineering journals: II. Mechanical engineering." *American documentation*, 10: 135-137, April 1959.

Burton, Robert E.
"Citations in American engineering journals: III. Metallurgical engineering." *American documentation*, 10:209-213, July 1959.

1960

Burton, R. E. and R. W. Kebler
"The 'half-life' of some scientific and technical literatures." *American documentation*, 11:18-22, January 1960.

Raisig, L. Miles
"Mathematical evaluation of the scientific serial." *Science*, 131:1417-1419, May 13, 1960.

Weiss, Paul
"Knowledge: a growth process." *Science*, 131:1716-1719, June 10, 1960.

Westbrook, J. H.
"Identifying significant research." *Science*, 132:1229-1234, October 28, 1960.

1961

Kessler, Maxwell Mirton
"Technical information flow patterns." In: Western Joint Computer Conference, Los Angeles, 1961. *Proceedings*. Los Angeles, National Joint Computer Committee, 1961. pp. 247-257.

Tannenbaum, Percy H. and Bradley S. Greenberg
"JQ references; a study of professional change." *Journalism quarterly*, 38:203-207, Spring 1961.

1962

Bain, Reed
"The most important sociologists?" *American sociological review*, 27:746-748, October 1962.

Kessler, Maxwell Mirton
Analysis of bibliographic sources in a group of physics-related journals. Arlington, Va., Armed Services Technical Agency, 1962. 21p.

Raisig, L. Miles
"Statistical bibliography in the health sciences." *Bulletin of the Medical Library Association*, 50:450-461, July 1962.
Tukey, John W.
"Keeping research in contact with the literature; citation indices and beyond." *Journal of chemical documentation*, 2:34-37, January 1962.

1963

Cole, P. F.
"Journal usage versus age of journal." *Journal of documentation*, 19:1-11, March 1963.
Garfield, Eugene
"Citation indexes in sociological and historical research." *American documentation*, 14:289-291, October 1963.
Garfield, Eugene and I. H. Sher
"New factors in the evaluation of scientific literautre through citation indexing." *American documentation*, 14:195-201, July 1963.
Kessler, Maxwell Mirton
"Bibliographic coupling between scientific papers." *American documentation*, 14:10-25, January 1963.
Kessler, Maxwell Mirton
"Bibliographic coupling extended in time: ten case histories." *Information storage and retrieval*, 1:169-187, November 1963.
Price, Derek J. D.
Little science, big science. New York, Columbia University Press, 1963. pp. 65-82.

1964

Garfield, Eugene
"Science citation index—a new dimension in indexing." *Science*, 144:649-654, May 8, 1964.
Garfield, Eugene
"Citation indexing; a natural science literature retrieval system for the social sciences." *American behavioral scientist*, 7:59-61, June 1964.
Garfield, Eugene, Irving H. Sher and Richard J. Torpie
The use of citation data in writing the history of science. Philadelphia, Institute for Scientific Information, 1964. 75p.

1965

Broadus, Robert N.
"An analysis of references used in the 1960 Encyclopedia of Educational Research." *Journal of educational research*, 58:330-332, March 1965.
Kaplan, Norman
"The norms of citation behavior: prolegomena to the footnote." *American documentation*, 16:179-184, July 1965.

Kessler, Maxwell Mirton
"Comparison of the results of bibliographic coupling and analytic subject indexing." *American documentation*, 16:223-233, July 1965.
Kessler, Maxwell Mirton
"The MIT technical information project." *Physics today*, 18:28-36, March 1965.
Price, Derek J. D.
"Networks of scientific papers." *Science*, 149:510-515, July 30, 1965.
Webb, Eugene J. and Jerry R. Salancik
"Notes on the sociology of knowledge." *Journalism quarterly*, 42: 591-595, Autumn 1965.

1966

Bayer, Alan E. and John Folger
"Some correlates of a citation measure of productivity in science." *Sociology of education*, 39:381-390, Winter 1966.
Sher, Irving H. and Eugene Garfield
"New tools for improving and evaluating the effectiveness of research." In: Conference on Research Program Effectiveness, 2d, Washington, 1965. *Papers*. Edited by M. C. Yovits, et al. New York, Gordon and Breach, 1966, pp. 135-146.

1967

Broadus, Robert N.
"A citation study for sociology." *American sociologist*, 2:19-20, February 1967.
Cole, Stephen and Jonathan R. Cole
"Scientific output and recognition; a study in the operation of the reward system in science." *American sociological review*, 32:377-390, June 1967.
Garfield, Eugene
"Primordial concepts, citation indexing, and historico-bibliography." *Journal of library history*, 2:235-249, July 1967.
Margolis, J.
"Citation indexing and evaluation of scientific papers." *Science*, 155: 1213-1219, March 10, 1967.
Meadows, A. J.
"The citation characteristics of astronomical research literature." *Journal of documentation*, 23:28-33, March 1967.
Parker, Edwin B., William J. Paisley and Roger Garrett
Bibliographic citations as unobtrusive measures of scientific communication. Palo Alto, Calif., Institute for Communication Research, Stanford University, 1967. 70p.
Stoddart, D. R.
"Growth and structure of geography." *Institute of British Geographers, Transactions*, No. 41, pp. 1-19, June 1967.

Xhignesse, Louis V. and Charles E. Osgood
"Bibliographical citation characteristics of the psychological network in 1950 and in 1960." *American psychologist*, 22:778-791, September 1967.

1968

Cole, Stephen and Jonathan R. Cole
"Visibility and the structural bases of awareness of scientific research." *American sociological review*, 33:397-413, June 1968.

Martyn, John and Alan Gilchrist
An evaluation of British scientific journals. London, Aslib, 1968. 51p. (Aslib occasional publication, no. 1.)

Oromaner, Mark Jay
"The most cited sociologists: an analysis of introductory text citations." *American sociologist*, 3:124-126, May 1968.

1969

Brown, Julia S. and Brian G. Gilmartin
"Sociology today; lacunae, emphases and surfeits." *American sociologist*, 4:283-291, November 1969.

Craig, J. E. G.
"Characteristics of use of geology literature." *College and research libraries*, 30:230-236, May 1969.

Earle, Penelope and Brian Vickery
"Social science literature use in the UK as indicated by citations." *Journal of documentation*, 25:123-141, June 1969.

East, H. and A. Weyman
"A study in the source literature of plasma physics." *Aslib proceedings*, 21:160-171, April 1969.

Lin, Nan and Carnot E. Nelson
"Bibliographic reference patterns in core sociological journals, 1965-1966." *American sociologist*, 4:47-50, February 1969.

MacRae, Duncan
"Growth and decay curves in scientific citations." *American sociological review*, 34:631-635, October 1969.

Price, Derek J. D.
"The structures of publication in science and technology." In: Gruber, William and Donald G. Marquis, eds. *Factors in the transfer of technology*. Cambridge, Mass., Massachusetts Institute of Technology Press, 1969, pp. 91-104.

Vickery, Brian C.
"Indicators of the use of periodicals." *Journal of librarianship*, 1:170-182, July 1969.

Whitley, Richard D.
"Communication nets in science: status and citation patterns in animal physiology." *Sociological review*, 17:219-233, July 1969.

Wood, David N. and Cathryn A. Bower
"The use of social science periodical literature." *Journal of documentation*, 25:108-122, June 1969.

1970

Cole, Jonathan R.
"Patterns of intellectual influence in scientific research." *Sociology of education*, 43:377-403, Fall 1970.

Cole, Stephen
"Professional standing and the reception of scientific discoveries." *American journal of sociology*, 76:286-306, September 1970.

Garfield, Eugene
"Citation indexing for studying science." *Nature*, 227:669-671, August 15, 1970.

Garfield, Eugene and Anthony E. Cawkell
"Repartee." *Journal of library history*, 5:184-188, April 1970.

Line, Maurice B.
"The 'half-life' of periodical literatures: apparent and obsolescence." *Journal of documentation*, 26:46-54, March 1970.

Price, Derek J. D.
"Citation measures of hard science, soft science, technology, and non-science." In: Nelson, Carnot E. and Donald K. Pollock. *Communication among scientists and engineers*. Lexington, Mass., Heath, 1970, pp. 3-22.

Stewart, June L.
"The literature of politics; a citation analysis." *International library review*, 2:329-353, July 1970.

Velke, Lissa
"The use of citation patterns in the identification of 'research front' authors and 'classic' papers." In: American Society for Information Science. *The information conscious society; proceedings of the 33rd annual meeting of ASIS*. Washington, 1970. pp. 49-51.

1971

Broadus, Robert N.
"The literature of the social sciences: a survey of citation studies." *International social science journal*, 23:236-243, 1971.

Cole, Jonathan R. and Stephen Cole
"Measuring the quality of sociological research; problem in the uses of the Science Citation Index." *American sociologist*, 6:23-29, February 1971.

Lehnus, Donald J.
"JEL, 1960-1970; an analytical study." *Journal of education for librarianship*, 12:71-83, Fall 1971.

1972
    Crane, Diana
        Invisible colleges; diffusion of knowledge in scientific communities.
        Chicago, University of Chicago Press, 1972. 213p.
    Fletcher, John
        "A view of the literature of economics." *Journal of documentation,* 28:283-295, December 1972.
    Garfield, Eugene
        "Citation analysis as a tool in journal evaluation." *Science,* 178:471-479, November 3, 1972.
    Lehnus, Donald J.
        "Who cited what? A citation analysis of the four basic cataloging texts." *Journal of the American Society for Information Science,* 23: 100-108, March-April 1972.
    Miller, Elizabeth and Eugenia Truesdell
        "Citation history; history and applications." *Drexel library quarterly,* 8:159-172, April 1972.

BIBLIOGRAPHY

Bayer, Alan E. and John Folger. "Some correlations of a citation measure of productivity in science." *Sociology of education*, 39:381-390, Winter 1966.

Broadus, Robert N. "The literature of the social sciences: a survey of citation studies." *International social science journal*, 23:236-243, 1971.

Earle, Penelope and Brian Vickery. "Social science literature use in the UK as indicated by citations." *Journal of documentation*, 25:123-141, June 1969.

Garfield, Eugene. *The use of citation data in writing the history of science.* Philadelphia, Institute for Scientific Information, 1964. 75p.

Kessler, Maxwell Mirton. "Technical information flow patterns." In: Western Joint Computer Conference, Los Angeles, 1961. *Proceedings*. Los Angeles, National Joint Computer Committee, 1961. pp. 247-257.

Lin, Nan and Carnot E. Nelson. "Bibliographic patterns in core sociological journals, 1965-1966." *American sociologist*, 4:47-50, February 1969.

Lubetzky, Seymour and R. M. Hayes. "Bibliographic dimensions in information control." *American documentation*, 20:247-252, July 1969.

Price, Derek J. D. "Citation measures of hard science, soft science, technology." In: Nelson, Carnot E. and Donald K. Pollock. *Communication among scientists and engineers*. Lexington, Mass., D. C. Heath, 1970. pp. 3-22.

Price, Derek J. D. "Networks of scientific papers." *Science*, 149:510-515, July 30, 1965.

Rawski, Conrad H. "Subject literatures and librarianship." In: Bone, Larry Earl, ed. *Library school teaching methods; courses in the selection of adult materials*. Urbana, University of Illinois, 1969. pp. 92-113.

Stone, Lawrence. "Prosopography." *Daedalus*, Winter 1971. pp. 46-79.

Weintraub, Melvin. "Citation indexes." In: *Encyclopaedia of library and information science*. New York, Marcel Dekker, 1971. vol. 5, pp. 16-40.

Weiss, Paul. "Knowledge: a growth process." *Science*, 131:1716-1719, June 10, 1960.

Westbrook, J. H. "Identifying significant research." *Science*, 132:1229-1234, October 28, 1960.

Xhignesse, Louis V. and Charles E. Osgood. "Bibliographical citation characteristics of the psychological journal network in 1950 and in 1960." *American psychologist*, 22:778-791, September 1967.

INDEXES

All personal, corporate, and other proper names in the text, notes, tables, lists, and appendices have been indexed. Each name is followed by the page numbers where it appears or is discussed. No indication is given if the name appears more than once on the same page, which is quite often the case.

The "General Index" includes names of institutions, associations, government agencies, conferences, corporate authors, titles of publications without personal authors (e.g., Prussian instructions, Library journal, etc.), awards, etc. Subordinate bodies (e.g., branch libraries, committees and divisions of associations, university libraries, etc.) have not been indexed separately under their own names if the name of the parent body is required for their identification, but they are included in the references given for the higher body.

The "Personal Name Index" contains the names of all persons discussed or mentioned; personal authors of works about these persons; and the personal authors of all works cited, used, or otherwise listed in this study. All corporate authors are listed in the "General Index."

GENERAL INDEX

American Association for the Advancement of Science, 101
American Library Association, 14, 23-24, 26-27, 29, 34-39, 41, 43, 56, 58-59, 66-68, 70-71, 75, 79, 88, 93-94, 96, 113
Amherst College, 31, 35-36, 39

Bermondsey Public Library, 33
Biblioteca Vittorio Emanuale, 61
Bibliothèque Nationale, 32, 34
Birmingham Public Libraries, 61
Bodleian Library, 15, 94, 113
Boston Atheneum, 31-32, 34-36
Boston Public Library, 31, 34, 39
Bournemouth Public Library, 39
Bradford distribution, 77, 79
British Museum, 4, 14, 27, 30-31, 44, 59, 61, 66-70, 86, 95, 105, 113
Bromley Public Libraries, 34

Brooklyn Public Library, 33, 38-39, 72
Brown University, 30
Bruce Free Library, 38
Burton-upon-Trent Public Library, 33

Cambridge University. Library, 96, 113
Catalogers' and classifiers' yearbook, 23-25, 79
Chelsea Public Libraries, 32
Classification Research Group, 60, 63
Clerkenwell Public Library, 32
Cleveland Public Library, 37-38
College and research libraries, 25
Columbia College. School of Library Economy, 36, 86
Columbia University, 37, 44-45, 48, 50-55, 57, 60, 86-87

Comité International des
Bibliothèques, 5th, Berne, 1932,
59
Committee for the Study of Cost
Accounting in Public Libraries, 60
Congrès International des
Bibliothécaires et des Bibliophiles,
Paris, 1923, 34, 41
Coventry Public Library, 34
Croydon Public Libraries, 32-34, 39,
44, 86

Dartmouth College, 37
Dartmouth College Library bulletin,
25
Denmark. Bogsamlingskomite, 97,
113

École des Bibliothécaires, 54
Edinburgh Public Libraries, 34

Government Printing Office, 24, 26,
79
Great Britain. Parliament. House of
Commons, 95

Harvard College, 31, 35-36
Harvard University, 39, 44-45, 48,
50-53, 87

Indianapolis Public Library, 37
Institute on Catalog Code Revision,
McGill University, 1960, 58, 110
Institute on Catalog Code Revision,
Stanford University, 1958, 15, 24,
58, 94, 96, 98-101, 114
International Conference on Cataloguing Principles, Paris, 1961, 58,
60, 63
International Congress of Librarians,
Chicago, 1893. *See* World's Columbian
Exposition, Chicago, 1893.

International Federation of Library
Associations, 15, 62, 101, 105,
114
International Library Conference,
1st, London, 1877, 32, 40
International Library Conference,
2d, London, 1897, 32, 40, 59
Islington Public Library, 33, 44
Italy. Direzione generale delle
accademie e biblioteche, 15, 66,
68, 71, 101, 114

John Crerar Library, 36, 38, 87
Journal of cataloging and classification, 23-25, 79
Journal of documentation, 25

Kölner Stadtbibliothek, 62
Königliche Bibliothek, Berlin, 62
Kungliga Biblioteket, Stockholm,
102, 114

Lancashire County Library, 87
Lenox Library, 38
Librarian and book world, 25
Library Association, 14, 32, 34,
56, 88, 94, 114
Library Association record, 24
Library Bureau, 35
Library journal, 24-25, 35, 74, 79
Library of Congress, 14, 26, 33,
37, 39, 44-45, 50-51, 53-55, 57, 60,
66, 68, 71, 86-88, 102-103, 114
Library quarterly, 24-25, 79
Library resources and technical
services, 23-24
Library trends, 25
Libri, 25

Manchester Public Libraries, 33
Margaret Mann Citation in Cataloging
and Classification, 55-58, 61, 88
Medical Library Association, 8, 11

130

Milwaukee Public Library, 35
Music Library Association, 105, 114

National Liberal Club, 32
New York Free Circulating Library, 38-39, 53, 78
New York Library Club, 38
New York Public Library, 33, 37-39, 44-45, 47, 50-53, 55, 57, 87
New York State Library, 37
New York State Library School, 32-33, 35-38, 42, 54-55, 60, 73
Newark Free Public Library, 35
Newton [Mass.] Free Library, 34
Norsk bibliotekforenig, 105, 114

Ormskirk County Branch Library, 87
Ousterhout Free Public Library, 35

PNLA quarterly, 25
Pacific Northwest Library Association, 60
Paris Library School, 54
Peterborough Public Library, 32
Philadelphia Free Library, 33
Pittsburgh Public Library, 33
Princeton University, 86
Prussian instructions, 14, 66, 68, 70-71, 106, 114

Readers' and Writers' Economy Company, 35
Royal Society Library, London, 32

St. Agnes Free Library, 38
St. Louis Public Library, 35
San Francisco Public Library, 35
Science citation index, 1, 5
Sorbonne, 61

Spain. Junta Facultativa de Archivos, Bibliotecas y Museos, 109
Spain. Junta Técnica de Archivos, Bibliotecas y Museos, 16, 108, 115
Spelling Reform Association, 42

U.S. Bureau of Education, 70, 97
U.S. Department of State. Division of Geography and Cartography, 60
Universität Göttingen, 32, 59
Université de Paris. *See* Sorbonne.
University College, London, 34
University of California, Berkeley, 44, 46, 50-51, 53
University of Chicago, 24, 26, 29, 37, 44-46, 50-55, 57, 61, 79, 86-87
University of Durham, 32
University of Illinois, 45, 49-51, 53, 60
University of London, 8, 60, 87
University of Michigan, 44, 47, 50-51, 53-55, 57, 59, 86-87
University of North Carolina, 44, 47, 50-51, 53-54, 86
University of Wisconsin, 60

Vatican Library, 14, 66, 68, 71, 109-110, 115
Vereinigung Berliner Bibliothekare, 59

Wallasey Public Libraries, 33-34
Wesleyan University, 37
Western Joint Computer Conference, Los Angeles, 1961, 121, 127
Western Reserve University, 38
Wilson library bulletin, 25
World's Columbian Exposition, Chicago, 1893, 32-33

Yale University, 45, 49-53

Zeitschrift für Bibliothekswesen und Bibliographie, 25

Zentralblatt für Bibliothekswesen, 25

PERSONAL NAME INDEX

See the note on page 129 for information on the index.

Acomb, Henry Waldo, 32, 40, 107, 113
Adair, W. C., 120
Adams, Winona J., 53, 59, 60, 63, 93, 113
Akers, Susan Grey, 14, 46-47, 50, 55-56, 66, 68, 72-73, 81, 83-84, 89, 93, 113
Allen, Edward S., 117
Allez, George Clare, 15, 48, 50, 60, 66, 68, 74, 81, 83, 93, 113
Alvord, Dorothy Maria, 48, 50, 60, 93, 113
Angell, Richard Sloane, 46, 49-50, 58, 60-61, 81, 83-86, 94, 113
Arnold, Denis Victor, 59-60, 81, 86, 94, 113
Ash, Lee, 52
Atherton, Pauline, 58

Bain, Reed, 121
Baldwin, Emma Virginia, 53, 59-60, 63, 94, 113
Ball, Katherine L., 63
Banay, George L., 119
Barnard, Cyril C., 118
Barrett, Mildred, 120
Barrett, Richard L., 120
Bauhuis, Walter, 61-62, 94, 113
Bayer, Alan E., 123, 127
Berthold, Arthur B., 15, 47-48, 50, 81, 85, 94, 113
Bishop, William Warner, 14, 45, 47, 50, 54, 56-57, 59, 66, 68, 72-73, 80-82, 84-86, 94, 113
Boggs, Samuel W., 53, 59-60, 62, 95, 113

Bone, Larry Earl, 5, 127
Borome, Joseph A., 31, 39
Bostwick, Arthur Elmore, 15, 38-39, 45, 52, 56, 81, 84, 95, 113
Bower, Cathryn A., 125
Branscomb, B. Harvie, 47, 50, 81, 84, 95, 113
Broadus, Robert N., 76, 120, 122-23, 125, 127
Brodman, Estelle, 119
Brown, Charles Harvey, 120
Brown, James Duff, 14, 32-34, 40, 44, 66, 68, 72-73, 75, 81, 83, 95-96, 113
Brown, Julia S., 124
Buelow, Bertha E., 53, 59, 62, 96, 113
Burch, Vella Jane, 47, 50, 81, 84, 96, 113
Burton, Robert E., 121
Butcher, Stanley J., 59-60, 81, 86, 96, 113
Butler, Pierce, 57

Carnovsky, Ruth French. *See* Strout, Ruth French.
Casey, Albert E., 119
Cawkell, Anthony E., 125
Chaplin, Arthur H., 15, 56, 59-61, 66, 68, 75, 81, 84-86, 96, 113
Childs, James Bennett, 15, 45, 50, 66, 68, 72, 81, 84-85, 96, 113
Cole, Dorothy E., 52
Cole, Jonathan R., 123-25
Cole, P. F., 122
Cole, Stephen, 123-25

Colvin, Laura C., 47, 49-50, 56, 81, 84-85, 96, 113
Coney, Donald, 15, 46-47, 50, 59, 81, 84, 96, 113
Cook, Dorothy E., 52, 101-102
Craig, J. E. G., 124
Crane, Diana, 54, 57, 126
Croft, Kenneth, 119
Crosno, C. D., 117
Crunden, Frederick, 35
Currier, Thomas Franklin, 14, 38-39, 48, 50, 81, 84, 96, 113
Custer, Benjamin, 16, 46, 48, 50, 61, 81, 84-85, 97, 113
Cutter, Charles A., 14, 27, 31-32, 34-36, 45, 52, 56, 65-67, 69-70, 73, 81, 83, 89-90, 97, 113
Cutter, William P., 39

Dalziel, Charles F., 118
Dawe, Grosvenor, 31, 36, 39, 41-42
Dean, Hazel, 15, 47-48, 50, 66, 68, 74, 81, 85, 97, 113
Delisle, Leopold, 15, 32, 61, 81, 83, 97, 113
Dewey, Melvil, 14, 31-37, 42, 45, 52, 54, 56-57, 60, 66-67, 70, 80-83, 86, 97-98, 113
Dunkin, Paul S., 15, 49-50, 56, 60-61, 66, 68, 75, 81, 84-86, 98, 113
Dziatzko, Karl, 15, 32, 59, 62, 81, 83, 98, 113

Earle, Penelope, 76, 124, 127
East, H., 124
Edwards, Edward, 21, 30-31, 44, 98, 113
Ellinger, Lucile M. *See* Morsch, Lucile M.
Ellinger, Werner B., 15, 45, 48-50, 60, 81, 84-86, 98, 113
Ellsworth, Ralph E., 15, 46, 50, 81, 84, 98, 113

Esdaile, Arundell J. K., 56, 59, 61, 98, 113

Fagan, Louis, 30-31, 39
Fairthorne, Robert A., 2, 5, 18, 77
Fellows, Jennie Dorcas, 14, 37, 42, 45, 50, 66, 68, 72-73, 81, 83, 98, 113
Field, F. Bernice, 49-50, 56, 99, 113
Fletcher, John, 126
Fletcher, William Isaac, 15, 35-36, 39, 41, 53, 56, 66, 68, 74, 76, 81, 83-84, 89, 99, 113
Folger, John, 123, 127
Foskett, D. J., 40-41, 43
Francis, Sir Frank C., 56, 59-61, 81, 84-86, 99, 113
Frels, Wilhelm, 15, 61-63, 66, 68, 74, 99, 113
Friis, Th., 120
Fry, Walter G., 40
Fuchs, Hermann, 16, 59, 99, 113
Fumagalli, Giuseppe, 27, 61, 69, 99, 113
Fussler, Herman H., 119

Garfield, Eugene, 5-6, 120, 122-23, 125-27
Garrett, Roger, 123
Gifford, Florence M., 38, 53, 99, 113
Gilchrist, Alan, 124
Gilmartin, Brian G., 124
Gjelsness, Rudolph H., 15, 17, 47-48, 50, 54, 59, 81, 84-85, 115
Goodrich, Nathaniel L., 37, 53, 81, 83, 110, 113
Graesel, Arnim, 15, 59, 62, 66-67, 71, 89, 99, 113
Greenberg, Bradley S., 121
Gregory, Jennie, 118
Gross, E. M., 117
Gross, P. L. K., 117
Gruber, William, 124

Gull, Cloyd Dake, 15, 46-47, 50, 60, 81, 84-86, 99, 113

Hackh, Ingo, 118
Hagedorn, Ralph K., 53, 59-60, 99, 113
Hand, Elinor, 46, 50, 81, 85, 100, 114
Hanson, James C. M., 14, 37, 39, 45-46, 48, 51, 54, 57, 66, 68, 72, 74, 80-86, 100, 114
Hart, Hornell, 117
Haskins, Susan M., 14, 47-48, 51, 81, 84-85, 100, 105, 114
Hayes, R. M., 7-8, 11, 127
Haygood, William C., 46, 51, 81, 84, 100, 114
Henkle, Herman H., 15, 29, 46-47, 49, 51, 61, 80-87, 100, 114, 118
Herrick, Mary D., 49, 51, 100, 114
Hesse, Leopold A. C., 21, 61, 100, 114
Hickox, Elinor Hand. *See* Hand, Elinor.
Hill, Frank P., 35
Hiss, Sophie K., 37-38, 53, 82-83, 100, 114
Hitchler, Theresa, 14, 38-39, 53, 66, 68, 72-73, 75, 78, 89, 100-101, 114
Hooker, Ruth H., 118
Howe, Harriet E., 16, 46, 48, 51, 82, 84, 101, 114

Jackson, Frederick, 34
Jackson, Sidney L., 49, 51, 82, 85, 101, 114
James, Hannah P., 35
Jast, L. Stanley, 15, 17, 32-34, 40, 56, 80-83, 86, 115
Jenkins, R. L., 117
Jewett, Alice L., 52
Jewett, Charles C., 14, 21, 27, 30-31, 35, 39, 53, 62, 66-67, 69, 79, 101, 114

Joeckel, Carleton B., 96
Johnson, Margaret F., 37, 42, 53, 101-102, 114
Jolley, Leonard J., 14, 59-60, 82, 86, 102, 114
Jones, J. Winter, 31
Josephson, Aksel G. S., 15, 36, 38, 45, 52, 82-83, 102, 114

Kaiser, Rudolf, 15, 61-62, 66, 68, 74, 102, 114
Kaplan, Norman, 122
Kebler, R. W., 121
Kessler, Maxwell M., 76, 121-23, 127
Keysser, Adolf, 61-62, 102, 114
Kingery, Robert E., 15, 17, 48, 51, 55, 82, 85, 115

Landau, Thomas, 52, 63
Lane, William Coolidge, 16-17, 32, 35-36, 39, 45, 52, 56, 82-84, 115
Ledos, Eugene, 34, 102, 114
Lehnus, Donald J., 5, 125-26
Lewis, Dorothy C., 49, 51, 60, 62, 95, 114
Lin, Nan, 76, 124, 127
Linderfelt, Klas A., 15, 35, 41, 53, 56, 58, 66-67, 70, 82-83, 103, 114
Line, Maurice B., 125
Lipetz, Ben-Ami, 9, 12
Lock, Reginald N., 72
Lockridge, Lillian L., 118
Louttit, C. M., 118, 120
Lubetzky, Seymour, 7-8, 11, 14, 24, 27, 29, 46, 51, 54-55, 57, 60-61, 65-66, 68, 75-76, 80-87, 90-91, 103, 114, 127
Lydenberg, Harry M., 38, 42

McColvin, Lionel R., 40
MacDonald, M. Ruth, 15, 17, 48, 51, 55, 82, 84, 115
MacNair, Mary Wilson, 15, 36, 45, 51, 60, 66, 68, 75, 82-85, 103-104, 114

134

McNeely, J. K., 117
MacPherson, Harriet D., 15, 47-48, 51, 66, 68, 75, 82, 84-85, 104, 114
MacRae, Duncan, 124
Maire, Albert, 61, 104, 114
Mann, Margaret, 14, 38, 47, 51, 54-55, 57, 66, 68, 72-73, 76, 82, 84-85, 88-90, 104, 114
Marcus, William E., 53, 59-60, 63, 94, 114
Margolis, J., 123
Marquis, Donald G., 124
Martel, Charles, 15, 45, 51, 60, 82, 84-85, 104, 114
Martyn, John, 124
Mash, Maurice H. B., 33-34, 82-83, 104, 114
Meadows, A. J., 123
Mecklenburg, Hermann B., 61-62, 69, 104, 114
Mengert, William F., 118
Metcalf, Keyes D., 14, 17, 47-48, 51, 56, 59, 82, 84-85, 115
Milkau, Fritz, 102
Miller, Elizabeth, 126
Miller, Robert A., 14, 46, 48, 51, 82, 84-85, 104, 114
Minto, Charles S., 41
Mishoff, Willard O., 46-48, 51, 82, 84, 104, 114
Morgan, Melvin B., 121
Morsch, Lucile M., 14, 17, 45, 48-49, 51, 55-56, 82, 84-85, 88, 115
Mortimer, Russell S., 59-60, 82, 86, 104, 114
Mudge, Isadore G., 15, 37, 48, 51, 66, 68, 74, 82-85, 105, 114
Munford, William A., 32, 34, 40-41, 58

Nelson, Carnot E., 11, 76, 124-25, 127
Norris, Dorothy May, 16, 61, 78, 105, 114

Nyholm, Amy F. Wood, 14, 46, 51, 66, 68, 74, 82, 85, 105, 114

Oromaner, Mark Jay, 124
Osborn, Andrew D., 14, 47-49, 51, 54-55, 57, 60-61, 66, 68, 74, 76, 80-87, 105-106, 114
Osgood, Charles E., 76, 124, 127

Paisley, William J., 123
Palmer, B. I., 40-41, 43
Panizzi, Sir Anthony, 4, 16, 21, 27, 30-31, 44, 61-62, 65-67, 69, 79, 86, 90-91, 105, 114
Parker, Edwin B., 123
Parry, John H., 31
Patterson, Austin H., 118-19
Paulin, Lorna V., 56, 59-60, 78, 82, 86, 105, 114
Perkins, Frederic B., 34-35, 45, 52, 82-83, 106, 114
Pettee, Julia, 14, 49, 51, 66, 68, 74, 76, 106, 114
Phillips, Philip Lee, 45, 51, 82, 84, 106, 114
Pierce, Watson O'Dell, 53, 59-60, 63, 106, 114
Pierson, Harriet Wheeler, 14, 36, 45, 51, 66, 68, 75, 82-85, 106, 114
Piggott, Mary, 8, 11, 24, 59-60, 63, 78, 80-87, 94, 96, 99, 102, 104-106, 108, 110, 114
Pollock, Donald K., 11, 125, 127
Postell, William D., 119
Price, Derek J. D., 5, 9, 11, 64-65, 76, 122-25, 127
Prime, Laura M., 8
Prince, Thomas, 31

Quinn, John Henry, 14, 32, 40, 66, 68, 71, 82-83, 89, 106-107, 114

Raisig, L. Miles, 121-22
Randall, William M., 15, 24, 46-47, 51, 82, 84, 104, 107, 109-110, 114
Ranganathan, S. R., 14, 27, 34, 41, 56, 61, 66, 68, 71-73, 75, 82, 84-86, 107, 114
Rawski, Conrad H., 3, 5, 127
Reichmann, Felix, 46, 51, 82, 84-85, 107, 114
Rider, A. Fremont, 14, 36-37, 42, 53-54, 60, 66, 68, 74-75, 82-83, 107-108, 114
Rouveyre, Edouard, 61, 108, 114

Salancik, Jerry R., 123
Savage, Ernest A., 33-34, 41, 56, 82-83, 108, 114
Sayers, W. C. Berwick, 14, 33-34, 39, 56, 72, 82-83, 95, 108, 114
Schneider, Georg, 59, 108, 114
Sharp, Henry A., 14, 33-34, 66, 68, 72-73, 82-83, 108, 115
Sheppard, Oden E., 118
Sher, Irving H., 122-23
Sherwood, K. K., 117
Smith, Maurice H., 119
Spalding, C. Sumner, 15, 17, 46, 48, 51, 56, 61, 82, 84-86, 115
Stevens, Rolland Elwell, 120
Stewart, James D., 14, 32-34, 39-40, 43-44, 82-83, 108-109, 115
Stewart, June L., 125
Stoddart, D. R., 123
Stone, Lawrence, 4, 6, 127
Strout, Ruth French, 16, 47, 49, 51, 58, 61, 63, 82, 84-85, 109, 115
Swank, Raynard C., 15, 46, 51, 61, 66, 68, 75, 82, 84-85, 109, 115

Tait, James A., 4, 6, 9, 13, 18, 27, 29, 77
Tannenbaum, Percy H., 121
Taube, Mortimer, 14, 46, 51, 66, 68, 75, 83-85, 109, 115
Tauber, Maurice F., 14, 46, 49, 51, 55, 60, 66, 68, 75, 83-86, 109-110, 115
Thom, Ian W., 48-49, 51, 83, 85-86, 109, 115
Thorne, W. Benson, 40
Tolpin, J. G., 120
Torpie, Richard J., 122
Trotier, Arnold H., 15, 17, 49, 51, 59, 83, 85, 115
Troxell, Wilma, 8
Truesdell, Eugenia, 126
Tukey, John W., 122

Van Hoesen, Henry B., 46, 48, 51, 83-84, 109, 115
Velke, Lissa, 5, 125
Ver Nooy, Winifred, 15, 37, 46, 51, 66, 68, 75, 83-85, 110, 115
Verona, Eva, 15, 27, 59, 61, 78, 83, 85-86, 110, 115
Vickery, Brian, 76, 124, 127
Voight, Melvin J., 119

Wallace, Ruth, 15, 37, 42, 45, 52, 83-84, 110, 115
Watkins, David R., 49, 51, 110, 115
Watts, Thomas, 31
Webb, Eugene J., 123
Weintraub, Melvin, 9, 12, 127
Weiss, Paul, 76, 121, 127
Wells, Arthur J., 15, 59-60, 83, 86, 110, 115
Westbrook, J. H., 5, 121, 127
Weyman, A., 124
Wheatley, Henry B., 15, 32, 66-67, 70, 83, 110, 115
Whitley, Richard D., 124
Whittemore, Caroline, 37, 49, 51, 83, 85-86, 110, 115
Williamson, Charles C., 52

Wilson, Louis R., 15, 46-47, 51, 54, 56-57, 80-84, 86, 110, 115
Wood, Amy Fredericka. *See* Nyholm, Amy F. Wood
Wood, David N., 125
Woodford, A. C., 117

Wright, Wyllis E., 14, 48-49, 51, 56, 61, 66, 68, 74, 80-83, 85-87, 109-111, 115

Xhignesse, Louis V., 76, 124, 127